Situation Tactical

**Memoirs of World War II
Army Combat in the
European Theater of Operations**

by
Martin H. Curtis

DORRANCE PUBLISHING CO., INC.
PITTSBURGH, PENNSYLVANIA 15222

All Rights Reserved
Copyright © 2004 by Martin H. Curtis
No part of this book may be reproduced or transmitted
in any form or by any means, electronic or mechanical,
including photocopying, recording, or by any information
storage and retrieval system without permission in
writing from the publisher.

ISBN # 0-8059-6387-1
Printed in the United States of America

First Printing

For information or to order additional books, please write:
Dorrance Publishing Co., Inc.
701 Smithfield Street
Third Floor
Pittsburgh, Pennsylvania 15222-3906
U.S.A.
1-800-788-7654
Or visit our web site and on-line catalog at www.dorrancepublishing.com

Contents

Preface v
Acknowledgments vii
1. Attack East 1
2. Attack North 10
3. Extend Northwest 23
4. Defend at Rimling 34
5. Shifts 45
6. Remain in Place 55
7. Pursue Northeast 61
8. Capture Heilbronn 70
9. Attack South 76
Glossary 85
Bibliography 90
Appendix A: Geography
    Mapping 93
    France, Locations 95
    Germany, Locations 100
Appendix B: Organizations in WWII
    The 100th Infantry Division 101
    The 374th Field Artillery Battalion 103
    A Combat Infantry Battalion 103
    Battalion Tactical Units 104
Appendix C: A Battle for Heilbronn
    Proposal for Citation 105
    Statement of Richard Drauz 113
Lists
    Topics List 115
    Locations List 116
    Personnel List 118

Preface

The original account was closed at Fort Still, Oklahoma, in October, 1946. It remained among the author's belongings until 1994 when the news media recognized the fiftieth anniversary of the events of World War II. The manuscript was sought out and referred to in 1994 and 1995 to recall events a half a century earlier; the account was adequate for that purpose.

In 1995 a copy of Keith E. Bonn's study *When the Odds Were Even* was obtained. On trying to relate the contents of this compilation to the events in Bonn's study, it was found that more information was needed. The depth of the account was improved by using the material available in the references: the unit histories of the 374th Field Artillery Battalion, the 397th Infantry Regiment, and the 100th Infantry Division. Some useful information was also found in loose papers located with the manuscript.

The original text has been augmented to increase its value to the author and to anyone else who might read it. It had never been edited and contained errors of spelling, grammar, and usage. To retain the original flavor, it was edited but kept in its original form. The text of the memoirs was expanded by the addition of dates and mention of calendar events. Augmenting was done by using introductory material and by use of footnotes. Attachments were used to provide backup material not readily available after so many years.

It took special effort to keep from embellishing the original material and to keep its flavor as it was written. It is hoped that the augmenting material is based on facts and observations and that it does not contain opinions and judgment. The account was prepared when concern over censorship was still in mind; other contemporary concerns might flavor the account also.

The annotations contain supplemental data on personnel, terrain, and military organizations. No attempt was made to include photographs. Few are known that are specific to the account, but the referenced unit histories have photographs that are pertinent. It is recommended that anyone reading this account also read the cited references, which contain much related material.

To really bring this account to life would require many sheets of maps and wartime overlays. The range in which we moved was defined on a 1:25,000 scale. The maps seen in other accounts of activities reported in this memoir have been

PREFACE

found to be based on the ones actually used during combat, and thus are suitable to be used to follow it.

The account begins the first day of combat for the author. At the time he is the communications officer/headquarters battery commander of the 374th Field Artillery Battalion. The organization was a truck-drawn battalion of 105 mm howitzers, part of the 397th Combat Team 100th Infantry Division. Subsequently he became a liaison officer and accompanied the 2nd Battalion, 397th Infantry. The account ends on VE Day. Conditions were *Situation Tactical* for six months.

The matters set forth here are autobiographical in nature. This is not a history of any group or organization but only the memoirs of one individual as he performed his various duties. Most of it is from the battalion level viewpoint, and big picture strategic matters are only introduced to tie happenings to better known events, places, and dates.

The account should be read with the understanding that it is, as represented, recollections of combat—nothing more. The writing was started two months after VE Day as a compilation of facts and incidents that the writer wished to have on file in an orderly sequence before they were entirely forgotten and as an activity to relieve the monotony of the Army of Occupation.

Events are reported as correctly as possible. Many of them were checked against unit records; however, the author left the Army of Occupation before he had finished compiling the account. Every effort was made to keep dates, persons, and places properly recorded, but the accuracy does not equal that of a day-to-day diary.

You are invited to share this account of the writer's combat experiences in the European Theater of Operations in World War II.

Acknowledgments

The author wishes to acknowledge the aid and support he has received in issuing this annotation. This extends to those who provided sources, helped with research, aided in clerical tasks, and supported the author through the time he was occupied with it.

Two archival agencies provided source material. The staff of The National Archives II, College Place, Maryland, were very helpful in finding wartime reports, journals, accounts, and those papers preserved by the army. The staff of The U.S. Army Military History Institute, Carlisle, Pennsylvania, likewise was invaluable for their help finding access to WWII vintage source material, manuals, and other published materials.

The 100th Infantry Division Association, its members, its newsletter, and its website have been helpful throughout the recent effort.

Two individuals have rendered great assistance with the effort. Brian Kopp, Glen Arm, Maryland, aided the research at Pennsylvania locations. Janie Ho Togia, of Issaquah, Washington, provided the secretarial and editorial aid necessary for the final issuance of the manuscript.

This annotation would not have been possible without the aid and support of my wife, Rowean. She translated French papers and reports, went on my tour of battle sites, and made it possible for me to find the space and time necessary for this effort.

CHAPTER 1

Attack East

The 100th Infantry Division entered the combat zone of the VI Corps early in November 1944 near the Meurthe River in the region of Lorraine in northwestern France. It joined the Seventh Army's attack on the German winter line in the High Vosges Mountains from the vicinity of Baccarat. It attacked along the Meurthe River southeast to Raon-l'Etape, thence northeast via N-424 and N-420 to Schirmeck. After this penetration of the German defensive and advancing into Alsace, the division was ordered to a new sector at the end of November. The author sees the action as the headquarters battery commander/communications officer of the 374th Field Artillery Battalion.

On Wednesday, 1 November 1944, the 374th Field Artillery Battalion closed in an assembly area near St. Helens, France, and established local security, and the preparation of individual protection was ordered. The slit trenches were neither numerous nor deep, however, when a sudden loud explosion was heard nearby. It was the sound of a battery of heavy artillery firing—sufficient to inspire more effort on digging of slit trenches. One of the more inquisitive men found the bodies of two German soldiers nearby—a bit putrid—which several more men visited; this was an introduction to what was to become a familiar sight. The drizzle added to the misery of what was to be our last pup-tent camp for some time.[1]

On the evening of 2 November our commanding officer, Lieutenant Colonel Claude M. Liles,[2] received orders to report to the commanding officer of the 158th Field Artillery Battalion (of the 45th Division) to receive instructions for our supporting them with our reinforcing fires. The next morning, 3 November, I joined the 374th FA Bn. reconnaissance party, and we proceeded to the village of St. Benoit, where firing battery positions and a battalion command post (CP) location were selected. After the CP was set up—very conveniently at the only road junction in the town—its location was changed to the edge of town. The battalion was moved into these locations, by infiltration, prior to noon.[3]

ATTACK EAST

Our first shot in combat was fired by Baker Battery, at about 1250, under control of an observer in the 45th Division artillery air observation aircraft. Soon Charlie Battery and the Able Battery followed, firing missions in that order. In the meantime I was visiting artillery communications officers, commos, of the 45th Division to see what tips they might have for me.[4]

In the afternoon low flying planes passed over the battalion area with everyone looking up at them and not taking cover. They were German ME-109s. Our first contact with the enemy air power passed without an exchange of fire either way. The next day the 1st Platoon, Baker Battery, 898th AAA Battalion (AW), a 40 mm AA organization, was attached to us. This began a long and pleasant association with them. During that day I also took Private First Class Jessie F. Gibson's stripe from him for firing a captured weapon carelessly.[5]

On the evening of 4 November, the 374th FA Battalion received orders to move to the vicinity of the city of Baccarat and to reinforce the 160th Field Artillery Battalion (45th Division). On the fifth the reconnaissance party started out at 0700. While reconnoitering we heard a deep roar and were able to see a large formation of friendly bombers on their way to Germany. The remainder of the battalion arrived by 1800 and was ready to fire, the necessary firing of registrations having been made by one howitzer from each battery that had accompanied the reconnaissance party.

Baccarat was noted for its crystal ware. Several of the members of the battalion made crystal purchases while we were there, but a lot of it did not get back to the United States intact. Our CP there was one of the better that we had in November, from the standpoint of comfort to the men, but it did lack adequate vehicle parking facilities and was high on a hill, possibly in sight of the enemy. Fortunately the enemy artillery was trying to knock out the Meurthe River Bridge in town and didn't shell us. This elevation also paid off later when high water made conditions bad for other installations.

On Sunday the sixth, a liaison section and forward observer parties joined the 3rd Battalion, 397th Infantry, and later in the day we sent similar representation to the 2nd Battalion, 397th Infantry.[6] Our battalion reconnoitered positions were never occupied. On 7 November we joined the 397th Infantry in our normal direct support missions, thus assuming our usual place in the 397th Combat Team. The 938th FA Battalion was attached to us to reinforce our fires.

On the eighth a heavy rain fell, making the firing battery positions very muddy and hindering operations. The 397th Infantry had relieved a regiment of the 45th Division, and other elements of the 100th were doing the same. On 9 November, at 0600, the 100th Division was completely on the line and functioning under the VI Corps. As the 100th Division's presence in combat was classified as Secret and to cover up the relief of the 45th Division, we copied all of the 45th's SOPs and particularly their SOI. (See Glossary for meaning of abbreviations.)

The front lines passed through Bertrichamps, where the church steeple was our favorite observation post and dug-in entrenchments around La Chique Farm were

ATTACK EAST

favorite targets. On the eighth, near the church, First Lieutenant Robert D. Smith[7] became the first casualty of the 374th FA when hit over the eye by a shell fragment.[8] He returned to duty with us about a month later.

The past few days had been quiet for us, enabling everyone to get settled into his combat jobs. Equipment was still catching up with us, and an SCR-193 (short wave radio-telegraph equipment) was finally pieced together. Considerable fuss was made over use of a recently received gasoline powered electrical generator for lighting in the fire direction center (FDC).

Orders were received on the evening of the tenth to prepare for an attack on the twelfth. Armistice Day, 11 November,[9] was not a time of truce in 1944 and just another Sunday in the war.[10] On the twelfth the 69th AFA Battalion was attached to us.

On 12 November, the 397th Infantry attacked at 0900 in the direction of Raon-l' Etape.[11] Before dark they halted, and we fired defensive fires for them.[12] The day was rainy, cold, and misty with poor visibility. Difficulty was experienced in maintaining radio communications. During the night a command car with radio operator and guard was set out on a hill, and by daylight radio communications had been established via relay to all elements of the battalion.[13]

Plans had been made for a coordinated attack in continuation of the previous day's advance. Just prior to the planned move-out of the 1st Battalion, 397th Infantry, the Germans attacked. Our liaison officer at the 1st Battalion, First Lieutenant Walter R. McGuire[14] called for preplanned fires and the infantry claimed that the Germans lost about 140 soldiers. As the result favorable progress was made with the attack after that.

The first snowfall of the season fell that day, making visibility poor during the morning. Reconnaissance was made for artillery positions in the vicinity of Bertrichamps. While on reconnaissance I saw a two and a half ton truck loaded with the bodies. The soles of their shoes identified them as American soldiers.[15]

On the fourteenth the battalion movement to positions near Bertrichamps was started. It soon became apparent that moving the firing batteries was a difficult process in the mud. Only Charlie Battery completed the move that day. After one tractor per battery were drawn from a supporting supply depot, firing battery movement was relatively easily accomplished the rest of the winter.

The command post (CP) did not move that day, and I stayed at the forward switching central overnight. I shared the switching central with First Lieutenant William E. Perry, Jr.[16] and the remainder of his forward observer party. They were adjusting to the loss of Technician Fifth Class Clyde Lull[17] who had been killed at about 1300 by a mortar shell. One of the Charlie Battery men refused an order to return with the FO party to the front. In the afternoon Second Lieutenant Anthony Christobek,[18] also of C Battery, was wounded by a mortar fragment in his leg. He eventually made it back to the States.[19]

The fifteenth was misty and visibility was poor.[20] It was the second anniversary of the activation of the division. The 397 Infantry was to wait for the 399th

Infantry to come abreast to their left. A counter-attack was driven back during the day by artillery fire. The 374th FA Battalion completed its move to Bertrichamps. This was one of the few times that the artillery and infantry command posts were boot-to-boot, as doctrine specifies. In digging latrines three bottles of good cognac were recovered in the garden. First Sergeant Charles W. Schlosser[21] took care of the headquarters battery officers—First Lieutenant William J. Slayline,[22] First Lieutenant John D. Lafferty[23] and myself enjoyed one of those bottles during the evening.[24]

On the sixteenth I picked up the headquarters battery payroll at the 100th Division Rear Command Post in Rambervillers. We had to pass over a refilled crater in the road west of Baccarat, blown days after we had taken over the area. The next few days were spent paying the first payroll in combat. We took most of it back in the form of payroll transfer accounts (PTAs) to be sent back home.[25] Also that day, the first officers' liquor ration arrived. During the day the 397th Infantry, moving behind a rolling barrage, frontally attacked the hill mass northeast of Raon-l'Etape and reached their objective.[26] The 397th commanding officer, Colonel William A. Ellis[27] was killed when his jeep was driven past our front lines. Weather: intermittent showers and snow.

The seventeenth, cold and clear, saw the German winter defense line around Raon-l'Etape completely broken.[28] A German ME-109 dropped two bombs nearby and then was chased away by planes of the Twelfth Tactical Air Force, who were on missions in our sector. The 69th AFA was released from its attachment to us.

On the nineteenth a friendly artillery shell landed in Able Battery's firing position. The 397th Infantry made little headway on the eighteenth (Sunday) and the nineteenth, but during the night of the nineteenth and twentieth they entered St. Blaise.[29]

On the morning of the twentieth, we reconnoitered for positions on the east edge of Raon-l'Etape.[30] Engineers were working in the town to remove mines from culverts, sewers, etc. While on reconnaissance Major Allen R. Green[31] and a wire crew captured the 374th FA's first prisoners. A forward switching center was established in Raon-l'Etape and functioned overnight. By noon of the next day the entire battalion had moved on to Raon-l'Etape. The CP and FDC were established in a tavern with a supply wire in the cellar and a good-looking brunette managing activities. A headquarters battery wire truck laying wire south of town struck a mine, injuring Private Warren G. Collins[32] and totaling the truck.

The twenty-second found us again preparing to move. A battalion area was selected between Moyenmoutier and Senones. While on reconnaissance I caught a ride, hanging on to the side of a 397th Infantry Jeep; I ended up falling off while the jeep was moving and was rather badly shaken up. We had reconnoitered on the tail of a marching infantry column, which wasn't too bad. When the battalion started to displace into the new area, however, the road was jammed with vehicles from a task force held up by a roadblock up ahead. After the CP was partly established in a large house and water mill, it was decided to move to a less conspicuous

ATTACK EAST

spot. This proved to be prudent later when high water made the house and mill untenable.

Lieutenant Lafferty, in charge of the 374th FA's graves registration team, removed the body of a dead German soldier from one of the firing battery positions.[33] My bruises started to get the better of me, so I went to the battalion aid station and they gave me some pain pills. It rained heavily that evening. Rather doped up, I spent the night on the hay in the barn with the switchboard crew and Staff Sergeant Richard J. Sullivan.[34] During the night I was aware of Technician Fifth Class Angelo DeSpirit[35] answering the calls with his deep throated, "Frog," our switchboard designation.

Thanksgiving Day, the twenty-third, was another rainy day. We had a restaurant for a mess hall and were served turkey with all the trimmings. The infantry made favorable progress and completed crossing the crest of the High Vosges Mountains into Alsace. I still didn't feel very well and did very little during the day. It was my turn to be battalion duty officer that night, however, so I stayed awake by censoring mail. When I went to bed I had better surroundings than the previous night; I slept in the message center shack, the domain of Sergeant Leon F. Bell[36] and Corporal Robert M. Willis.[37]

The morning of the twenty-fourth was a rainy, disagreeable morning. We reconnoitered while walking behind the infantry as they cleared the way. Major Greene and Captain Max Foster[38] captured six Germans in Plaine, where we located our CP. The major got a German P-38 pistol out of the episode. We had crossed Hantz Pass and found out that we were now in Alsace and that the civilians spoke a form of German.[39] The CP was located in a schoolhouse, and there was plenty of evidence of the Nazi training that the students had been getting. Only a short while ago a German officer had occupied the room in which the battery officers had slept. We found some fresh baked Wehrmacht bread and tasted it—not very good. During the day I saw a familiar face in a jeep on the road and thus encountered First Lieutenant Wendell Guthart. He was a captain when I met him again in Grenoble.[40]

On the twenty-fifth we found that we were reinforcing the 925th FA Battalion as the 399th Infantry went down the Bruche River Valley. We had no fire missions during the day. We had the 100th Division Counter Intelligence Corps (CIC) investigate individuals in the town whom we suspected of being Nazi sympathizers because they spoke German. There were no Nazi sympathizers found.

On the twenty-sixth we went through what could be called a rat race. Orders were to reconnoiter for positions in the vicinity of Still. The usual recon group went out, taking a howitzer from Charlie Battery and a jeep with a fifty-caliber machine gun mounted on it.[41] The HQ portion of the recon party left the C Battery portion in Urmatt. It was the first Sunday since Urmatt had been liberated, and there was a church service being held in a church adjacent to where the howitzer and machine-gun-carrying jeep were parked. When some German soldiers were seen near the town, the howitzer and machine gun opened fire. The churchgoers probably were wondering if their celebration was premature. A total of twenty-five prisoners were taken there later; they were probably part of the group of Germans who were attacked.

In the meantime we in the advanced recon party were having experiences of our own. Major Greene, Captain Skivington,[42] and myself were being offered *eau-de-vie* by every civilian who saw us in Flexburg. We soon received orders to return to the battalion. We found only a guide where we had left the battalion; they had started to move up when they received orders to go back to Raon-l'Etape and await new orders. The rest of the recon party went to Raon-l'Etape, but I stayed to look for two of headquarter's battery wire trucks that might not have received the orders. I spent several hours riding around, bucking all sorts of traffic, as the entire 100th Division was trying to leave the area and another division was trying to get into it. I finally went to Raon-l'Etape and found the battalion, after dark, in the same area we had previously occupied. The two "lost" vehicles were there with the battalion.

That day I had received a package of popcorn in the mail.[43] We tried to pop it in some "butter" from a 10-in-1 ration. Lieutenant Lafferty got his mess kit all gummed up, and we didn't have any popcorn. Freshly popped corn would have tasted very good on that rainy evening after a day of running around.[44]

Notes

1. Tent camps, or bivouacs, were only used in the field away from combat. In tactical situations, troops slept on the ground, in outbuildings, in vehicles, etc. In the United States, the third amendment to the Constitution prohibits "quartering." In friendly countries, such as France, troops were billeted with the citizens, and in enemy countries, such a Germany, civilians were ordered out and dwellings were utilized by United States troops.

2. Liles, Claude M., Lt. Col., initial CO 374 FA.

3. The military used the 2400-hour clock. In the ETO all the theater was standardized on double daylight time, based on the Greenwich median. Obviously this resulted in some deviations from solar time.

4. The 45th Infantry Division, a National Guard Division, had seen a lot of action in the Mediterranean area and seemed a good organization to ask questions about combat. Most impressive was the close relationship of the personnel due to their common hometowns and area; even after extensive turnover of personnel there was a strong cohesion based on common areas of origin and years of training together.

5. Gibson, Jessie F., Pfc., reduced to Pvt., HQ 374 FA, KIA.

6. The forward observer teams from Charlie Battery customarily accompanied the Infantry 3rd Battalion; Baker Battery FO teams went with the 2nd Battalion, etc.

7. Smith, Robert D., 1st Lt., FO, C 374 FA, later LnO 3, 374 FA.

8. Shell fragment is the proper designation for splinters of steel from the explosive burst of shell. A common mistake is to designate shell wounds as being made by shrapnel. The splinters gave much uglier wounds than the lead balls of WWI shrapnel shells.

9. An interesting Memorial Day coincidence occurred in the 398th Infantry sector. A reminder of WWII was encountered; it had the sign "American Expeditionary Forces Cemetery 1918." (See Hancock, Frank E., *An Improbable Machine Gunner*, 2nd Ed., Madison, AL, 1997.)

10. Combat operations were carried on every day of the week. Significant calendar dates have added to the text. Sundays are mentioned as a tribute to those who regularly found a Sunday worship service.

11. This attack was over the open fields of the valley of the Meurthe River and there was little cover from enemy observation posts in the nearby hills.

12. The 100th Division history, *The Story of the Century*, is very good about reporting the number of field artillery rounds fired during this period; it was discontinued later in that book. Data on casualties (and prisoners) are more significant and were available. The post-war histories—divisions, regimental, battalion, etc.—as well as these memoirs were written with post-action official reports available. These reports had full data in them, but we were not encouraged to use the data at the time. The details on battles and such found in the histories were based on the write-ups recommending unit awards and individual decorations. Examples may be found in Boston's *History of the 398th Infantry Regiment in World War II*.

13. The Century Division's experience in the Tennessee Maneuvers nearly a year previously paid off at this time; use of relay stations in mountains had been practiced then. The Vosges Mountains in the winter are much like the Cumberland Mountains in the winter, and thus we utilized other lessons we had learned then.

14. McGuire, Walter R., 1st Lt., later Capt., LnO 374 FA.

15. A rifle company account of the action occurring at this time is found in Bowman, B. Lowery, & Mosher, Paul F., *Company I—WWII Combat History*, Carrolton, Texas, 1997.

16. Perry, William E. Jr., 1st Lt., FO, C Btry. 374 FA.

17. Lull, Clyde, Tech 5, FO Party, C 374 FA KIA.

18. Christobeck, Anthony, 2nd Lt., FO, C 374, FA, WIA.

19. The 374th casualties, Smith, Christobeck, and Lull, were all Charlie Battery members. Since Charlie Battery FO parties were with the 3rd Battalion, their injuries were indicative of the difficulties that the 3rd Battalion of the 397th Infantry was encountering. (Bowman, B. Lowery, and Mosher, Paul F., *Company I—WWII Combat History*, Carrolton, Texas, 1997.)

20. *Beachhead News* (published by VI Corps). Tues., Nov 14, 1944, Weather Forecast. "Cloudy, intermittent snow; Colder, minimum temperature, 28 degrees."

21. Schlosser, Charles W., 1st Sgt., HQ Btry., 374 FA.

22. Slayline, William J., 1st Lt., Asst. Comm. O., 374 FA, KIA.

23. Lafferty, John D., 1st Lt., Motor O., HQ Btry. 374 FA.

24. Battery officers in the artillery (and company officers in the infantry) were held in greater esteem by the men in their units than were staff officers or other officers further from them. If not, the bottle would have gone to the battalion commander or would not have been shared with any officer. The last time that we three officers had a social drink together had been in New York City on the first of October. We had been on pass from Camp Kilmer, New Jersey, prior to embarking for Europe. At Billy Rose's Diamond Horseshoe we drank the only liquor available, Scotch whiskey, for which I didn't particularly care. Our November cognac tasted a lot like it. Later on I found out why: the Thirty Years War and the search for a cognac substitute.

25. This was our first pay with military scrip. We received US published paper money with franc values.

26. During this time other 100th Division elements were also making progress along their fronts. The 1st Battalion of the 399th Infantry won the first Distinguished Unit Citation for the division for their actions on November 16 and 17. They captured a hill mass known as Tete Des Reclos, which provided the enemy with observation of Raon-l'Etape and made any advance on the city potentially very costly. (Gurley, Franklin L., *Into the Mountains Dark: A WWII Odyssey from Harvard Chrisom to Infantry Blue*, Bedford, PA. Aegis 2001.)

27. Ellis, William A., Col., initial CO 397 Inf., KIA.

28. The town of Raon-l'Etape is shown as being taken by the 397th Infantry on 15 November in the *100th Division History*, although 18 November is probably a better date. The town claims that it was liberated by the 399th Infantry, which had circled around it. The Germans had abandoned the town, so technically the town had not been captured by any unit. For further information on the town and its war experience, see the appendix.

29. This small village of St. Blaise was two kilometers south of Raon-l'Etape, on N-59 and in Lorraine. Another St. Blaise is located on N-420, 30 kilometers by road east of Raon-l'Etape.

30. The west edge of Raon-l'Etape is the boundary between the two civil areas of the Vosges Region and the Meruthe and Moselle Region.

31. Greene, Allen R., Maj., S-3, 374 FA.

32. Collins, Warren G., Pvt. 374 FA, WIA.

33. A rumor that I later heard was that the corpse lost a ring finger prior to its disposal. By then it was too late for me to investigate.

34. Sullivan, Richard J., Staff Sgt., wire sect., HQ 374 FA.

35. DeSpirit, Angelo, Tech. 5, switchboard opr, HQ 374 FA.

36. Bell, Leon F., Sgt., msg. cen., and mail clerk, HQ 374 FA.

37. Willis, Robert M., Cpl., msg. cen., 374 FA.

38. Foster, Max W., Capt., S-2, 374th FA.

39. A recognized dialect, Alsatian German. Alsace had been part of Germany off and on over the centuries. We saw papers pasted on the walls that only said "YA!" presumably posted by the French underground to remind the Alsatians that they had voted in a plebiscite to join Germany in the late 1930s.

40. Guthart, Wendell, 1st Lt., later Capt., 405 FA Gp (from Charles City, Iowa).

41. Artillery reconnaissance parties often took a howitzer with them so that the registration of the battalion could commence. (Registration is the process of locating the howitzers in respect to target areas.) Some artillery Jeeps, including the one assigned to me, had mounts for fifty-caliber machine guns to be used for anti-aircraft protection.

42. Skivington, Capt., B 898 AAA.

43. An important part of the text of the mail home was nearly always a request for an item that the serviceman desired to be sent through the mail. The US Post Office would not take packages addressed to military personnel overseas without seeing a written request from the service man.

44. Officers' evenings in combat were not often available for popcorn parties or for sharing campaign as we had done on a previous evening. Much of the paperwork for a military organization is done by clerks and senior NCOs, but the papers had to be reviewed and signed by the responsible officer, usually at night. There were also plenty of letters that had to be censored.

CHAPTER 2

Attack North

At the beginning of December 1944, the Century Division, now part of the XV corps, was ordered to attack north from along the Moder River (Highway N-419) in the direction of the town of Bitche. The division's sector was in the wooded west slopes of the Low Vosges Mountains. Their mission became the reduction of the Maginot Line fortifications in the Ensemble de Bitche. The author starts new duties as the artillery liaison officer to the 2nd Battalion, 397th Infantry. The 397th Combat Team advanced to the north and took the town of Mouterhouse and then positions south of the town of Bitche. After the 398th Infantry had captured a Maginot Line fortress in the division sector, orders were received to change the division sector.

The 100th Division became part of the XV Corps on the morning of 27 November. The 397th Combat Team moved from the vicinity of Raon-l'Etape to the vicinity of Niderviller, south of Sarrebourg.[1] As the 374th FA Battalion was arriving in Plaine de Valsch, new orders arrived. After quickly eating noon chow, the reconnaissance parties moved out again. Saverne Pass had just been taken, and our combat team, attached to the 45th Division, was to assist in defending the north flank of the Allied penetration.

The 374th FA Battalion reconnaissance party proceeded to Dossenheim to receive orders from the 156th FA Battalion. The way up was difficult; traffic on the Sarrebourg-Saverne road was bumper-to-bumper. It was a good thing that we had air superiority. The side roads off the highway were littered with German equipment, abandoned in great haste as the Germans had been routed from the area. Children were playing around this equipment. A heavy fog was clinging to the woods and valleys, making the negotiation of curves and hills quite treacherous. Gun positions were selected at Ernolsheim, and I went back to meet the battalion to guide them forward.

We were released from attachment to the 156th FA Battalion and reverted back to our normal support of the 397th Infantry. That night it was my turn to be battalion duty officer for the first part of the night. I had a bit of difficulty getting off duty as the staff officer due to relieve me was billeted with a family that had locked their door for the night. The next day was the town's day to open all the cabbage fermentation crocks, thus sharing the entire strong odor as they had their weekly Alsatian sauerkraut feed.

The next morning, the twenty-eighth, the 374th FA Battalion's mission was changed to reinforcing the 45th Division Artillery, and we went off on reconnaissance. Battalion positions were at Niedersultzbach. Headquarter's battery kitchen truck had a flat tire on the move forward.

The command post was in a schoolhouse, very prominent on the top of a hill. Later, during the night of 2 December, the town received enemy artillery fire, but the only building that was hit was not this obvious target. A small building that the wire crew occupied was hit, with no damage done. The schoolteacher had left with the German army, leaving the Nazi school materials. She had lived in comparative luxury, which we enjoyed. The local civilians were looting her extensive wardrobe as we were moving in to the schoolhouse.

On 29 November my assignment was changed. Captain Robert G. Lind[2] was to become communication officer/headquarters battery commander, and I was to take his job as liaison officer-two, LnO-2.[3] The next few days were spent in turning command of the battery over to Captain Lind. Turning the LnO-2 job over to me was much less complicated. I had to prepare to travel light, and that was a time when I was receiving a batch of packages in the mail. During this time a series of mission changes ended when the 374th FA Battalion finally reverted to its normal mission, direct support of the 397th Infantry.

In the afternoon of Sunday, December second, I went to Ingwiller to the rear CP, 2nd Battalion, 397th Infantry and relieved First Lieutenant William E. Devereux,[4] who had acted as liaison officer when Captain Lind had gone to 374th FA Battalion HQ. There I joined the rest of the liaison section: Corporal Andrew J. Servas,[5] the chief-of-section; Technician Fourth Class Victor P. Bowler;[6] Technician Fifth Class Vincent A. O'Rourke;[7] Private First Class Gray M. Coggins;[8] and Private First Class Lewis R. Cooper.[9] Bowler was new to the section and was from B Battery. The others had been in HQ Battery with me for a long time.[10]

I stayed at the 2nd Battalion rear CP over night. I met two officers of the 2nd Battalion, Captain Herbert C. Newton[11] and Captain George I. Purington.[12] The morning of 3 December, I moved with the section to the forward CP in Rothbach, where I met First Lieutenant George N. McAllister.[13] The section extended our wire up to Rothbach, and we became part of the command post group. During the morning the town received a heavy concentration of light artillery and flak fire. In the afternoon I walked up to the 2nd Battalion front in the woods north of town, stepping over the body of a dead German officer. I contacted the forward observer parties and the 2nd Battalion commander, Major Wiley B. Wisdom.[14]

Later that day we learned that the remainder of the 100th Division had relieved the 44th Division to our left. We now were again in forested mountains. These

ATTACK NORTH

were the Low Vosges, and we were moving along them rather than across as we had done in the High Vosges.

That evening we received another heavy concentration of artillery and flak fire in Rothbach. The CP personnel retired to a potato cellar. We had front line companies giving us, "On the way," when the shells passed over them, and a couple of seconds later the shells would hit us.[15]

The shelling occurred when the 3rd Battalion kitchen deliveries were passing through town. One jeep received a direct hit while passing in front of the CP. After the shelling I was outside and wondered what a jeep was doing stopped in the middle of the road. Carefully covering my flashlight I looked over at the two figures sitting in the jeep and discovered the bodies of two men killed in the shelling.[16]

On the fourth of December the 2nd Battalion held up while the 3rd Battalion was attacking Hill 375, northeast of the Rothbach.[17] The defenders were well dug in, and the 3rd Battalion suffered several casualties;[18] however, the 3rd Battalion moved back and after artillery time-on-target (TOT) barrage they were able to take the hill. During this time I visited Captain Franklin J. Worth,[19] our liaison officer at the CP of the 3rd Battalion, 397th Infantry. The 2nd Battalion then had to overcome a roadblock; tanks were called to assist the engineers in this task. It was cleared without the tanks, however, by the engineers under First Lieutenant Raymon E. Denton.[20] It was discovered that the roadblock was at a position that gave a view down the road into town; that was probably the location of the OP for the artillery that had been shelling the town. It was a rainy, dreary day.

On the fifth the 2nd Battalion proceeded in the woods to the right of the Reipertswiller-Rothbach road with the supporting tanks advancing alongside of them on the road. When it became apparent that there was no opposition, the infantry left the woods and rode the tanks. That night the rifle companies were in, and the battalion CP was in Rothbach.[21]

On the sixth the 397th Combat Team reverted back to the 100th Division control with the mission of fighting its way back to our division to our left. The 2nd Battalion CP was moved to Reipertswiller, and plans were made to stay there for the night. The 374th FA Battalion also moved there from Schillersdorf. As soon as the 2nd Battalion was settled, it was ordered to proceed to Melch along with the 3rd Battalion. The 2nd Battalion ended the day dug in south of Mouterhouse, on Hill 335, with plans to attack in the morning. After a look at the terrain on foot, I returned to the rear CP at Melch for the night.[22]

The 2nd Battalion was due to jump-off for Mouterhouse at 0900 on the seventh. I went up to the forward CP early in the morning, checking the plans for the attack when the company COs were given their orders. At that time I learned that a two man enemy patrol had been fired on, killing one. The other, possibly an officer, had escaped. Our attack would lack surprise despite our precautions for a quiet approach.

Since moving, the 374th FA Battalion's guns had not been registered in their new position. I gave my section instructions for laying telephone wire and went,

ATTACK NORTH

with Tech 4 Bowler carrying our SCR-609 radio, to seek a vantage point from which to adjust registering fire. We had to pass through our own lines, which Bowler suspected and became very wary. By constantly assuring him, I finally got us to point about two hundred yards south of the village, where I had limited observation of a road junction. I started to register but never finished that mission as 0900 arrived and I had to cease fire to avoid any confusion with the flanking attack that I knew the 2nd Battalion was starting.

We were joined by First Lieutenant Carl H. Bradshaw[23] and some of his How Company (weapons company) men, and Bowler and I felt a little less by ourselves. Some time later the deployed riflemen of an infantry company passed through our position. Major Wisdom and his HQ party followed them. We used that position as on OP and a CP for the rest of the day. I acted as a radio relay station for Second Lieutenant Herbert R. Church,[24] the FO with the flanking company east of the village. He used the infantry radio to the 2nd Battalion CP, and I used our SCR-609 to the artillery FDC.

An enemy 20mm flak gun north of the town fired into the woods around us, but no damage was done.[25] By evening the infantry was in town mopping up, and my crew extended our wire into Mouterhouse and stayed with the infantry there. I returned in my jeep, and we slipped and slid our way back over the overburdened lumber trail to Melch. It had been a dreary day with some rain.

The eighth of December was the anniversary of the United States' declaration of war with Japan. That morning my section completed the move to Mouterhouse, where I joined the forward CP.[26] The rifle companies had cleared out the village the previous evening and were fairly well set up. In one building letters and papers were found which indicated that the captured personnel of Able Company 398th Infantry had been evacuated through Mouterhouse. That company had been captured on 4 December at Wingen-sur-Moder.[27] Other units were already starting to converge on the village to get themselves suitably situated to operate from there during the continuation of the advance towards the Bitche area, which was now our division objective.[28]

That afternoon the infantry, while patrolling north of town, had a skirmish with an enemy group. The patrol leader came to the CP and pointed out of the window to the troublesome area. Staff Sergeant Peter C. Moynahan,[29] with me as his telephone operator, acted as FO from the CP, and with the help of everyone from the battalion CO on down (except me, I carefully kept out of it) very thoroughly covered the hill. The infantry then sent in a second patrol, which discovered vacated positions but no Germans. A while, later after our patrol had returned, the enemy gave the same area a heavy shelling. It would appear that the Germans thought our fires were in preparation for an attack and that they were going to catch our infantry before they could dig in on the hill. The village started to receive enemy artillery harassing fire, which continued for several days. During the day both rain and snow fell.

On Sunday the ninth, it looked like the 2nd Battalion was to have a quiet day.

ATTACK NORTH

My section joined me in the CP; they had been in a house some distance away. The liaison section had a suitable location in the CP area due to First Sergeant Carl A. Hoover.[30] Lieutenant McAllister received order promoting him to captain.

News that the regimental shower unit was to be moved into town was cheerfully received. The unit later moved out when they were nearly hit by enemy artillery. A burst of close artillery round shattered the windows of our CP in the schoolhouse. The 374th FA Battalion completed a move to Hasselthal. The 2nd Battalion CP personnel shared Major Wisdom's fruitcake—one of several that CP personnel received and shared during the month. I first met Captain John P. Wilson,[31] then commanding George Company, and one of his officers, First Lieutenant John B. Richey.[32]

Our quiet day changed when orders came for us to move out, in the woods along the road north, the 3rd Battalion on the left of the road and the 2nd Battalion on the right. The rear elements of the 2nd Battalion came into Mouterhouse to take over the billets left as the others moved out.[33] The kitchens and motor sections were to regret the move when occasional enemy artillery rounds came into town. Regimental HQ had also moved into Mouterhouse and was in the center of impact for enemy artillery fires. We would call them to ask for shell reports—a reversal of the usual situation, which they didn't appreciate.[34] The 2nd Battalion progressed to their objective without difficulty and dug in for the night.

During the day I met Technician Fifth Class William F. Greci[35] and Private First Class Bernard C. Humphrey,[36] who were the drivers for the Baker Battery FOs who worked with me, and they eventually became almost part of our liaison section. The 2nd Battalion commo, First Lieutenant Edward D. Clark,[37] brought up his personal Hallicrafters radio receiver, which we were able to enjoy very much in the next few months.

On the tenth Brigadier General Maurice Miller[38] visited the CP. I was so surprised that I could not call, "Attention," but I do not recall any other visits of a general to the 2nd Battalion CP.

I had by now decided that Corporal Servas was not as aggressive as I thought a chief-of-section should be, although he was diligent, well-trained, and a loyal worker. When Captain Lind came up to pay us, Lind and I mutually agreed that Sergeant Kalman J. Chany[39] should join the section and be the chief-of-section and that Servas would serve as liaison corporal. When Chany arrived Pfc. Cooper left the section.

The 2nd Battalion was ordered to move up again on the tenth, which they did without much trouble. They were not too fortunate, however, as during the night the enemy crept into the edge of their position and carried away twenty How Company men as prisoners.[40] An enemy soldier who was captured after daylight said that they (the Germans) would have captured the entire battalion if the night has not ended so soon. The action did not end with the capture of some of the enemy. Jeeps carrying chow up a previously reconnoitered road were fired on by a flak-wagon, causing the convoy considerable confusion. The flak-wagon had been

ATTACK NORTH

abandoned the previous day but had not been neutralized. An enemy crew had reclaimed it, fired at the convoy, and then fled. Lieutenant Denton finally neutralized the gun.

Later that morning, the eleventh, I visited the 2nd Battalion companies on line, contacting their COs and "my" FOs.[41] Lieutenant Devereaux had a heavy beard, which I learned to expect him to grow every time he was up front as an FO.[42] Major Wisdom, feeling sick, returned with me to the rear CP, and Captain Newton took his place at the forward CP. It was rainy in the morning, but the weather cleared up in the afternoon. The evening was spent in helping to censor the mail of the 2nd Battalion HQ Company.

On the twelfth, Easy Company was moved out to Hill 333, straight north, after an artillery preparation. I wanted to get to that location by jeep, for some reason, so I took off to where they claimed to be. After a lot of dismounted searching for them,[43] I decided I had conquered a bit of territory for the United States Army with a lot of German telephone wire passing through it.[44] It had Pfc. Coggins wishing the he had been more careful to make sure he had his carbine with him; our only armament was my forty-five caliber Colt automatic. I found the area that had been shelled during the artillery preparation and noted a high percentage of tree bursts; there was no evidence of damage to the enemy. I contacted the 106th Cavalry Squadron, which was on our right (east) flank. I then located Easy Company, some distance west of where they were supposed to be. In my jeep I led them to where they belonged.[45]

On my way back to the 2nd Battalion CP, I found Lieutenant Slayline supervising the preparation of a dug-in position for the 374th FA Battalion CP near Peterphilippe—it never was used by the CP but became the 374th FA Battalion's aid station.

On 13 December, George Company returned to town for showers and rest in houses overnight. Major Wisdom returned to the forward CP. Captain Garden[46] returned to Easy Company, and First Lieutenant Heitman[47] returned to regimental HQ. In the afternoon I saw Technician Sergeant William Chase,[48] Staff Sergeant Roy S. Beach,[49] and Pfc. Fred Matts[50] pass the rear CP in a jeep. They told me that the Military Police had set up one-way traffic control but that they knew a short cut back to the 374th FA CP, which they were taking.

Shortly after I headed back to the 374th FA Battalion CP along the way that they had taken, over a little used road. We came upon their blown-up jeep; it had hit a road mine on the supposedly mine-cleared road. The remains of another jeep that had been blown up earlier were still beside the road.

I hurried on to the 374th FA Battalion CP and arrived as the men were being loaded into an ambulance. Sergeant Chase and Private Matts returned to the unit, but Sergeant Beach's combat days were over. Unfortunately that was not Matt's last road mine. My previous requests for sand bags in the floors of the liaison section jeeps were fulfilled after this incident. The day was cloudy and cool.

15

ATTACK NORTH

On the fourteenth Easy Company was relieved by George Company and returned to the village for showers and a night of rest. The 2nd Battalion made no other moves that day.

On the fifteenth the 2nd Battalion was ordered to move out. I started my crew laying wire, showing them an important short cut. I followed the battalion in our other jeep until they reached the objective; it was a tall hill, Hill 326, and overlooked what appeared to be a small lake.[51] While the infantry were digging in, I helped my men, who were struggling with our wire. We finished just before dark. As the men had not brought sleeping bags, I sent them back to the rear for the night but stayed with forward CP myself.

The W-130 wire that the infantry crew had laid along the route of movement was not working when darkness arrived; the W-110 wire[52] our section laid along the short cut was working. The 2nd Battalion CP was located in a large hole with a covering of logs (it was not even light-proof) that had evidently been prepared years earlier.[53] The dugout was big enough for ten to twelve of us to lie down for the night. All I had for warmth was the field coat I was wearing—and it was not very warm—as I lay on the hard, cold, damp ground. I would not have slept even if I had been warm, however, as I was trying to keep hold on the phone crank so that the phone would not ring. To add to the difficulties, we kept getting calls for information that we could only furnish using lights. It was my first night in the woods near the front and not a comfortable experience.

In December the nights are long and the days short. We were able to have two hot meals a day with 10-in-1 rations acting as the third. By combining the ingenuity of the How Company officers, Captain Anthony J. Maiale[54] and First Lieutenant John C. Noel,[55] with 10-in-1 rations and Christmas packages, we were able to be eating most of the time during daylight hours.

In the next few days the spirit of the approaching Christmas was evidenced by the decoration of a small evergreen tree near the CP; bits of color were provided by Christmas wrappings of gifts received in our packages and by the aluminum strips of chaff[56] laying about the area. The relative quiet of this period let me get to know many of the infantry CP personnel—Staff Sgt. Max Foreman[57] and Staff Sgt. Michael Ruggerio[58] were only two. I learned that triangular bandages could be used as handkerchiefs from Staff Sergeant Samuel Armstrong[59] of the medics.

On the sixteenth the section joined me at the battalion forward CP and installed themselves in two foxholes about fifty yards from the CP dugout where I was. They brought my roll, and the infantry kitchen jeeps brought up additional blankets so that we would be able to keep warm at night. The CP dugout was improved and made light-proof, so we could use lights in it.

In the afternoon of Sunday the sixteenth, the 2nd Battalion was to secure the next height, Hill 355, as a potential location from which to observe our present objective, Camp de Bitche. A patrol that went out was fired on and had one man mortally wounded; enemy fire prevented the evacuation of his body during daylight.

Plans were then made to send one company up the hill, following a time-on-target (TOT). We extended my telephone wire to an OP, then found out that there was not time to set up the TOT. We settled on a battalion concentration of fire. Captain Foster, who had come up to check on the observation possible when the objective was taken, joined me. In adjusting the fire I had one shell burst in a tree in front of the OP. This was not the way to establish a good reputation among the front-line infantrymen. The hill was taken, along with two prisoners. The observation of Camp de Bitche was nil, but I did get my first view of the Citadel and Town of Bitche. The hill did prove of value the next few days for observation in our sector.[60] Our wire was extended to an FO on the hill. On our return from the hill, Captain Foster and I were pinned down in the open by German artillery fire; it was a frightening experience and one that I would not choose to repeat.

That afternoon, around chow time, it became evident that the Germans knew where we were as we received the first of several shellings near the CP. Most of the men had prepared sufficient protection, but some AT Platoon men were away from their holes and received injuries.

It was cold and clear on the seventeenth. In the late morning the 2nd Battalion made feint towards Camp de Bitche to draw attention away from the 100th Division's main effort on the Maginot Line forts west of Bitche. The feint consisted of artillery and mortar fires and racing of tank motors. I visited by FOs, and we completed our wire to them. This gave us our first complete wire net. With a switchboard and a radio in the section foxholes and a telephone to me in the CP, we had minimized our communication problems, and that was the set-up we always tried to achieve in future static situations.[61]

The German artillery interdictory fires were a nuisance, knocking out the wires to the FOs. Sergeant Chany and Tech 5 O'Rourke did wonders repairing breaks under shellfire and at all times of the day and the night. One day they found a shell hole where they had sat to make a splice the previous day. They would go out, without orders, even when the infantry would order their linemen not to go out on the infantry line breaks; thus, our lines were frequently used by the infantry. Sergeant Chany was reported to talk in his sleep about these missions. I saw both Chany and O'Rourke each got a Bronze Star for their efforts.[62]

On 18 December the emphasis was on trying to get complete shell reports as the 397th CP in Mouterhouse and two batteries of the 374th FA Battalion at Peterphilippe were receiving harassing artillery fire. I visited Baker Battery with Tech 4 Bowler and then the 374th FA Battalion CP at Chile, near Mouterhouse. It was cloudy and rained a few times. A patrol was sent east from Hill 355 and returned with prisoners. After a search and questioning at the 2nd Battalion CP, during which they showed various stages of fear, the prisoners were sent to the rear making remarks about the Americans being good to them. One of them was a youth who had only started to shave; he cried when his razor was taken from him.

The nineteenth was a sunny day for a change, and we crawled out of our holes to enjoy the welcome warmth. Major Wisdom and Captain McAllister went to

ATTACK NORTH

Mouterhouse; Captain Newton came up to the forward CP to run the battalion. We started hearing of a German attack up north.

The twentieth was a foggy day. Our life had become almost routine in that static position. A short round of artillery fell in one of the company positions and killed one rifleman. Captain Foster came up, and we investigated it while getting hostile stares. It was established that the round was fired by the 397th Infantry Cannon Company.[63] I visited our FOs and the company commanders returning to the CP in time to prepare for something to eat and to read the daily distribution before hitting the sack. Major Wisdom and Captain McAllister had returned, and Captain Newton went to the rear.

On the twenty-first the 106th Cavalry Squadron alerted us to prepare to move upon relief. During one of the enemy's harassing artillery fires, about 1000, Sergeant Chany suddenly burst in the CP to tell me that Corporal Servas was injured. Getting two medics from nearby (they were a bit reluctant to go out in a shelling), we went to the foxhole shared by Servas and the others. A burst of an artillery shell outside the well-protected hole had sent one fragment into the hole, striking the switchboard and sending metal switchboard part flying into his back above his right kidney. The medics bandaged his wound and procured a stretcher for him. He died while being carried to the aid station about one hundred yards away. While on my way to the aid station to discuss the incident with the medical officer, Captain Leslie Zieve,[64] I was caught in another shelling and took refuge in a partially completed hole with no cover. I did quite a bit of thinking and sweating at that time.[65]

The section equipment had been damaged by the shell burst that had killed Corporal Servas. I had the men load up our belongings, and we went to Mouterhouse, reported Servas's death to Major Flemstead Coleman,[66] picked up my monthly liquor ration, and went to the 2nd Battalion CP. I had the section reload our equipment, segregating Servas's belongings and getting replacements for equipment damaged. I gave the men my bottle of Scotch whiskey; they were quite shaken by Servas's death and went to a nearby church to pray for him. While they were so occupied I learned the details of our next move.

Notes

1. This move was from the Lorraine Region to the Alsace Region.

2. Lind, Robert G., Capt., Liaison O, later Comm. O., 374 FA.

3. This change of assignment meant that my Military Occupational Specialty (MOS) went from 1200 to 1930. My designation on the telephone went from Frog 10 to Frog 242—the 374th telephone designator was Frog. The telephone designation of the 2nd Bn., 397th Inf. was Frolic White.

4. Devereux, William E. III, 1st Lt., FO, B 374 FA.

5. Servas, Andrew J. Jr. Cpl., Ln. Sec. 374 FA KIA.

ATTACK NORTH

6. Bowler, Victor P., Tech. 4, radio operator, B 374 FA.

7. O'Rourke, Vincent P., Tech. 5, wireman, Ln. Sec. 374 FA.

8. Coggins, Gray M., Pfc., driver, Ln. Sec. 374 FA.

9. Cooper, Lewis R., Pfc., later Cpl., Ln. Sec. 374 FA.

10. A liaison section was authorized to consist of a liaison sergeant, a liaison corporal, a driver, a radio operator, and a wireman/telephone operator. Its function was to extend the FA battalion communications (messenger, wire, and radio) to the liaison officer and the forward observers in the infantry battalion sector.

11. Newton, Herbert C., Capt., later Maj., Ex. O., 2nd Bn. 397 Inf.

12. Purington, George I., ("GI") Capt., 2nd Bn. 397 Inf.

13. McAllister, 1st Lt., later Capt., S3, 2nd Bn. 397 Inf.

14. Wisdom, Wiley B., Maj., later Lt. Col., CO, 2nd Bn. 397 Inf.

15. The time-of-flight information here indicates that this was howitzer fire. Artillery howitzers shells have an arched flight path needed to go over hills and down into woods, as we were at the time. Artillery guns fire high velocity shells on a flat trajectory and are most useful on flat open terrain and for penetrating armor or thick dense fortifications.

16. A night or two later, when I was censoring letters, I deleted parts with a vivid description of the scene the next day which portrayed the chickens pecking at the brains scattered on the road. I also omitted mention of this event in my original memoirs, even though they were written after the war. Censorship of such horrors of war, military movements, dates of actions, etc., results in personal accounts based on letters home being distorted from reality.

17. Hill heights in meters. Some hill masses had names, which were not given on tactical maps. The hill names were not used in lower unit communications, since numbers were less confusing. Hill names appearing in some accounts were added when they were prepared using material found in higher-level reports based on maps not used at the front. Since the area we were operating in was the Vosges Mountains, it might have been appropriate to name each peak and call it a mountain and not a hill. Indeed it would not take much for anyone who climbed those steep "hills" to believe that they were mountains.

18. Bowman and Mosher *op. cit.*, give a vivid description of the 3rd Battalion action between Ingwiller and Rothbach.

19. Worth, Franklin J., Capt., LnO 374 FA.

20. Denton, Raymon, 1st Lt., platoon leader, A 325 Eng., KIA. (The 2nd Platoon, Able Co., 325th Engineers normally supported the 2nd Bn., 297th Inf.)

21. I am sure that we smoked cigars in the 2nd Battalion CP that night. I was a pipe and cigar smoker at that time and had cigars shipped to me on a regular basis from a factory in Florida. Major Wisdom was also a cigar smoker and occasionally received them in a package from the States. We both bartered our issue of cigarettes to those around us for their issue of cigars.

19

22. My duties as a liaison officer were to keep the artillery informed as to the location of the infantry battalion elements and to pre-plan artillery fires to be used if needed for defensive or offensive actions. These had to be coordinated with infantry plans and transmitted, often as over-lays to infantry and artillery units. I could do this in the rear CP as well as the forward one.

23. Bradshaw, Carl H., 1st Lt., Mtr. Plat., H 397 Inf. KIA.

24. Church, Herbert, Jr., 2nd Lt., FO, B 374 FA.

25. The fire of 20mm flak into dense woods is very frightening to anyone in the woods. The shells have very sensitive fuses and burst on contact with only a leaf or a twig. The noise of the bursting shells in every direction and the small bits of steel shell casings flying around are cause for concern.

26. At the south end of Mouterhouse a stone monument marks the boundary between Alsace and Lorraine of some time ago; modern maps show the boundary near Melch. We had passed from the Bas-Rhin Department in the Moselle Department.

27. Personal mail could give quite a bit of information of intelligence value, and soldiers who otherwise observed rules about security still carried personal mail into combat. Accounts of this capture are given by Norman, Caldon R., *Whatever Happened to Company A?*, Portland, OR, 1991, and by Watson, William C., *First Class Privates*, Atlanta, GA, 1994.

28. The area of Bitche contains several locations with Bitche in their name. These included the town of Bitche, the Citadel de Bitche, the College de Bitche, and the Ensemble de Bitche. These are discussed in more detail in the appendix. The division objective was initially the Ensemble de Bitche, a sector of the Maginot line.

29. Moynahan, Peter C., Staff Sgt., later 2nd Lt., FO B 374 FA.

30. Hoover, Carl A., First Sgt., HQ Co. 2 397 Inf.

31. Wilson, John P., Capt., CO G 397 Inf.

32. Ritchey, John B., 1st Lt., G 397.

33. Mouterhouse was the only village of any size in the 397th sector, making it a choice place for rear-echelon installations. It also was an obvious target for German artillery interdiction fires. It had a population of three hundred in 1996.

34. Shell reports were to be made by all units that had evidence of enemy artillery activity. It consisted of any clues that could be use to determine the location of the enemy guns. The information sought was time, number of rounds, direction of sound of guns, sound of shells passage, etc.

35. Greci, William F., Tech. 5, FO driver, B 374 FA.

36. Humphreys, Bernard C., Pfc., FO driver, B 374 FA POW.

37. Clark, Edward O., 1st Lt., Comm. O., 2 Bn. 397 Inf.

38. Miller, Maurice, Brig. Gen., Asst. CG 100 Div.

39. Chany, Kalman J., Sgt., Ln. Sec., 374 FA. Sergeant Chany was then in Service Battery but had started out with Headquarters Battery. He had been in the AA/AT Platoon of Headquarters Battery when it was eliminated, but as the result of a personal

injury that incurred at the Port of Embarkation, he was not shipped with them but was returned to the 374th. With a non-authorized military occupation specialty, he was retained in the battalion.

40. My original version of this says twenty men from How Company. The 397th History says that eighteen out of twenty How Company were captured. The 100th Division history says that a section of machine guns and seventeen men were there, that all were gone except for one soldier who had been killed, and that the guns were still in place.

41. I find in my original memoirs I use the first person possessive about those near me. The FO parties really were members of Baker Battery, and as a battalion staff officer I only had limited control of them. Also, my original manuscript called them parties, a term that I choose to continue; it helps to prevent confusion with the liaison section. Properly they were FO sections.

42. I was familiar with Lieutenant Devereaux's heavy dark whiskers as he had served with me in headquarters battery earlier that year. He spent most of his time as FO, not asking for relief but allowing his party members to rotate. He was a favorite FO with the infantry companies. (Fishpaw, Eli, & Fishpaw, Bernice, *The Shavetail and the Army Nurse*, Deland, FL, 1988).

43. The word "dismounted" caught my eye as I was transcribing the original memoirs. It was a holdover from my training with horse-drawn artillery in ROTC. It looks like I still had some remaining traces of having been a "red leg" in me when I first wrote the memoirs!

44. German field telephone wire was single strand with an orange outer insulation. It was not often left on the ground when they moved—they were very thorough about picking it up. In this case we were apt to have been spotted by a German wire pick-up crew.

45. Under the heavy cover of the forest areas there are few terrain features to aid in guiding troop leaders in making movements.

46. Garden, William A., Capt., CO, Co. E 397th.

47. Heitman, Fred F., 1st Lt., later Capt., G Co. 397th.

48. Chase, William, Tech. Sgt., Comm. Chief, HQ 374 FA, WIA.

49. Beach, Roy S., Staff Sgt., Radio Sgt., HQ 374 FA, WIA.

50. Matts, Fred, Pfc., driver, HQ 374 FA, WIA (2).

51. Later it was seen that the body of water was one of several reservoirs formed by damming up the head of the Horn River. At one time the Horn River at the base of the Bitche Citadel formed a swamp, and a well inside the fortress could pump water up to besieged troops. Loss of the Horn's flow to diversion resulted in drying up both the swamp and the well.

52. The US Army field telephone wire was made up of twisted pairs of black insulated wire. The W-110 wire was heavy duty with a core of twisted strands of steel and copper conductors; it usually was laid from vehicles. The W-130 wire was much lighter in weight, and it was made for laying from hand-held reels.

ATTACK NORTH

53. Bonn's study states that the Germans prepared such field fortifications remaining in the vicinity before the French capitulated in 1940.

54. Maiale, Anthony J., Capt., CO H 397 Inf., later Maj., Regt S-3, 397 Inf.

55. Noel, John C., 1st Lt., MG platoon leader, H 397 Inf.

56. Chaff was name given to the metallic aluminum strips dropped by allied aircraft to mislead German radar.

57. Forman, Max, Staff Sgt., Intel. Sgt., later 2nd Lt., 2 397 Inf.

58. Ruggerio, Michael, Staff Sgt., Opns. Sgt., 2 387 Inf.

59. Armstrong, Samuel B., Staff Sgt., Med. Det. 2 397 Inf.

60. The best observation around was that the Germans had from the top of the Bitche Citadel. Because Bitche is surrounded by wooded hills higher than the Citadel, most observed artillery fire had to be directed by ground observers.

61. The radios could be made to operate remotely by use of a "black box" that permitted the operation of the radio by a field telephone.

62. They received only Bronze Stars and never received other awards for later actions, as it seemed that others should receive their first award before a second would be given. There were two types of Bronze Stars. Those awarded for Valor has a V device on their ribbon. Those awarded for Meritorious Service wore a bare ribbon. After the war it was proclaimed that all who had the Combat Infantry Badge also were awarded Bronze Stars.

63. Neither Major Wisdom, the battalion commander, nor I, the artillery liaison officer, had been informed of plans for Cannon Company fire in our sector. As part of my job was to keep friendly fire from hitting behind our line, this made me look bad.

64. Zieve, Capt., Leslie, Med. Det. 397 Inf.

65. I had not experienced fear during the shelling after Servas was killed—I had something to do. In this shelling I had mortality in mind and no activity to take my mind off of the shelling. This time shelling in the woods gave airbursts as well as ground bursts; this was a third dimension compared to the shelling that Captain Foster and I shared earlier in an open area.

66. Coleman, Flemstead L., Maj., Ex. O., 374 FA; later 1st Lt., 375 FA.

CHAPTER 3

Extend Northwest

On 21 December the Seventh Army spread out along the front to free up the Third Army so they could help contain the German offensive in the Ardennes. The 397th Infantry moved from the right to the left of the 100th Division; it moved from wooded forests to open fields. The regiment was greatly extended in a northwesterly direction from the rest of the division. The mission was to defend the present front, which was astride the Maginot Line and the French-German border. The author accompanied the 2nd Battalion, 397th Infantry, which was extended across the regimental sector as the Outpost Line of Resistance. On Christmas day enemy pressure caused the withdrawal of the OPL, exposing the other battalions on the Main Line of Resistance. The 2nd Battalion reverted to the reserve. On New Year's Eve a major German offensive was initiated. Most of the Seventh Army was forced to fall back, but the 397th Infantry held out around the village of Rimling. On 5 January, 1945, the 2nd Battalion was ordered into Rimling.

Due to the German offensive in the Ardennes[1] the Third Army, on our left, was moving up to the north to assist in countering the action up there, and the Seventh Army was extended to cover the front that the Third had been holding. This meant that we were to cease offensive operations and go into a defensive mode—the first time that the 100th Division had had to do that since it entered combat. The initial plan was for the other two combat teams to hold about the same sectors that they had been operating in while the 397th Combat Team was to move from the division right flank to its left flank.

Our movement started the afternoon of 21 December, the shortest day of the year. As maps were scarce and I had one set of the few available to the 2nd Battalion, I arranged to lead Lieutenant Clark and his 2nd Battalion communication men up ahead of the rest of the battalion. We went to Kleinmuhl, passing Maginot Line fortification in the area.[2] Shortly after dark the relief of the 1st Battalion, 114th

EXTEND NORTHWEST

Infantry, 44th Division was completed. The 2nd Battalion of the 397th was in reserve. The 374th FA Battalion firing positions were nearby. Across a gully from the CP was Able Battery, and blasts from their guns broke windows in our CP building. South of the village, Lieutenant Devereaux had the unique situation of being both with his infantry company and his assigned Baker Battery. The 397th was in reserve.

As the situation was defensive, on the morning of the twenty-second I took most of the men in my section on a terrain walk with Major Wisdom, inspecting the digging-in of the battalion in their defensive positions. I remember very clearly that it was very cold. In this defensive situation two artillery OPs were set up and manned.

On Sunday the twenty-third, the section was shuffled around as the result of the death of Corporal Servas. The remainder of his personal belongings was taken to HQ Battery, now located in Petit Rederching. In place of Servas, Private Donald Pine[3] joined the section at his and my request. We had Private First Class William Von Hegel[4] temporarily replacing Tech 4 Bowler, who had gone back to Baker Battery for a rest. Later in the day Private First Class Coggins and Tech 5 O'Rourke, shaken by Servas's death, went back to HQ Battery for a rest. As we were leaving the area, Private First Class Charles Cortellino[5] came up as their temporary replacement.

In the afternoon orders were received for a further spread of sectors, and under these new orders the 2nd Battalion was to form an OPL and the rest of the 397th Infantry to prepare a MLR on favorable ground in the rear. We set out to move to a new CP location in Rimling, but we received word on the way to go to Guiderkirch. The CP was set up in a house next to the church. The battalion arrived after dark and relieved elements of the 87th Division. That night Major Wisdom and others, inspecting the area we had taken over, went into Germany; the border passed through our sector.

The twenty-fourth was a clear cold day.[6] Major Wisdom, with his staff and the company commanders, went on a walk over the ground in front of our positions. Sergeant Moynahan and I were the artillery representatives in the group. After we had walked a ways into the woods on the left of our sector, I stopped and asked Moynahan to point out our position on the map, which he did. I then asked him if there was anything unusual about it, but he did not think so. I then pointed out the border. We shook hands as the first members of the 374th FA Battalion to get into Germany.[7] We then joined Major Wisdom and his party on the walk along the width of our sector. We were a small, compact group walking on ridgelines—what a target we would have been for the Germans, but we saw no signs of enemy or enemy activity. Later that day Cortellino and Pine crossed into Germany while laying a wire to Moynahan's OP.

During the day a partial issue of white winter parkas was made to the infantry company supply sergeants to replace the OD overcoats that the front line infantry

EXTEND NORTHWEST

had. That evening several of the officers came to the CP to celebrate Christmas Eve, but I crawled under a table and went to sleep. Others spent it much differently.[8]

Christmas Day 1944 was very cold, but clear, with good visibility. Early in the morning Sergeant Moynahan started calling back fire missions on enemy troops. The 374th FA Battalion FDC would not fire the missions, telling us that they were not sure the troops were not friendly.[9] Captain Foster, in good S-2 fashion, came up to the battalion CP, and I walked him up to the OP. After we had verified that the troops were enemy, we could only get a little artillery fire on them as most of the artillery in the sector was too far back. While observing that fire I saw for the first time the nature of Posit fuses.[10]

The town of Guiderkirch received a couple of concentrations of enemy artillery fire, so that the enemy knew where we were. During one of these shellings, Private Pine was on his way to the CP from where the section was staying when he had to dive for cover. He dove into one of the numerous manure piles found in the towns of this sector. The only damage from the shelling was a tear in his field jacket, but he was a mess![11] The only casualty of the shelling was an infantryman killed while digging his foxhole when a grenade in his belt exploded.

The troop movements observed from the OP and the shelling of the village should have tipped somebody off that the enemy was up to something, but we were ordered to expand our sector by relieving elements of the 12th Armored Division on our right. A company commander's meeting was called for 1530, and everyone started to enjoy his Christmas dinner—turkey, etc.—which arrived at 1430. Fox Company was digging in and didn't get started on the dinner right away, and the acting regimental commander arrived just before the company commander's meeting. Captain William Stallworth[12] arrived and stated that he had met the 44th Reconnaissance Troop (on our left) as they were moving out of position after having seen some German troops in the woods to our left. At this same time Second Lieutenant Preston Chambliss[13] who had relieved Sergeant Moynahan, called a fire mission on those woods. Then calls from Fox Company reported that they were being fired on from their left rear. At this time the acting regimental commander ordered the OPL to withdraw. The fire mission was not completed. In about two minutes troops were moving through town towards the rear, and by 1600 only my section and myself were left. I waited until both of the two FO parties arrived, loaded them—I do not know how—on our jeeps and, doubling the infantry column, went into Guising where the infantry were assembling.

It was interesting to note the change of attitude of the residents of Guiderkirch. They had been very friendly towards us, speaking French. When the movement out of town started, they stood in small groups, giving us dark looks and talking together in German. Several of the men put bundles on their backs and fell into the rear of the columns leaving town.

The 2nd Battalion was ordered to stay in Guising that night. The men of Fox Company were hungry as their chow trailer lacked a jeep to pull it when they

EXTEND NORTHWEST

pulled back. Also, several of the men had abandoned their newly issued snow parkas. After getting my facilities set up, I rode back in the dark to the 374th FA Battalion CP, now located in Bining, and discussed the situation with Colonel Liles and his staff. I went back to Guising, had a can of the beer we had just picked up from HQ Battery, and retired in my sleeping bag in what was left of a roofless room in a demolished house. It had been an interesting, if not a festive, Christmas!

On the twenty-sixth it was still very cold. The 2nd Battalion moved to Petit Rederching and set up a CP in a tavern. The day was spent busily planning a combat patrol into Erching. It started out to be a company of infantry supported by a platoon of tanks. By evening, when the final orders were given, it was a platoon of infantry accompanied by an artillery FO. I made plans for Lieutenant Chambliss to be picked up in Guising (his company was still there) and for them to accompany the patrol. A plan of fires was made out in case the patrol leader or Chambliss would call for them. The patrol was to move out in the darkness of early morning and to return by daylight.

We got up early in the morning of the twenty-seventh, and I took my radio jeep and accompanied Major Wisdom's party so that I could hear any calls for fire and work in conjunction with his infantry radio. On arrival in Rimling I found that Chambliss was not there, so I took an SCR-609 and delegated Private First Class Cortellino to help me carry it.[14] I left Private First Class Cooper with the jeep and its SCR-610 with Major Wisdom's party. The patrol was lead by Second Lieutenant James Martin.[15]

Erching had several fires burning that had been set the night before by white phosphorous shells. After a slow and quiet approach to the town we could hear animals and human voices. The town civilians were fighting the fires. We went into the outskirts of the town, talked with the civilians, and decided not to search for enemy soldiers because daylight was nearing. We returned to Rimling by a different route, arriving just as it was getting light. Again, it was a cold morning, but the hiking and carrying part of the radio kept me warm. In Rimling Major Wisdom and I visited the 3rd Battalion CP to telephone the results of the patrol to regimental HQ. Little did anyone realize the part that location would play in our future.[16]

In returning to Petit Rederching I got on the wrong road and ended up in Gros Rederching. When I found the right road I went back to Guising, found Lieutenant Chambliss, and got his story on why he missed the morning patrol.[17] I then went to visit another FO whose party was digging in with the infantry south of Guising. I foolishly drove up to the position on the exposed hill with my jeep. Just as I started talking with them the Germans started shelling the area. I quickly got my men in the jeep and left. It was a careless act on my part that had exposed everyone on the hill to artillery fire.[18]

Later the same day, the 2nd Battalion moved again, this time to Rohrbach,[19] where the CP was set up in the office of the Burgermeister, next to the church. It was a nice set-up with plenty of space for everyone in the command post. It even

EXTEND NORTHWEST

had a separate dining room that served as an officer's mess—Private First Class William Moseley[20] took pride in keeping it presentable. There was another building used for officers quarters, but I chose to sleep in the CP with the duty officer so that I could catch both the infantry and the artillery phone calls during the night.[21]

The mission of the 2nd Battalion was to prepare plans for a counter-attack and to dig alternate positions along the Maginot Line fortifications to meet any possible enemy breakthroughs. The ground was frozen, the weather was very cold, and continuous work was required during daylight hours. The lot of the 2nd Battalion infantryman as not an easy one when his outfit was in reserve; however, the regimental shower unit moved into town, and the men were able to use it, as well as to be inside building after dark.

Major Wisdom had been an instructor of defensive tactics at the Infantry School, so we had our defensive area planned according to the textbook. It ended up with nineteen platoon areas prepared, and I had several FO positions prepared with telephone wire laid to them.

The twenty-eighth was again very cold. First Lieutenant William Oakman,[22] a MAC officer, joined the battalion's medical detachment and thus shattered the hopes that Staff Sergeant Armstrong would get battlefield commission in recognition of his outstanding work. Fox Company was placed in position west of Guising, forming our contact with the 3rd Battalion, 71st Infantry, 44th Division. A company commander's meeting was held in the evening, chiefly devoted to administrative matters.

The twenty-ninth, my birthday, was another cold, clear day.[23] We started receiving the British Broadcasting Company radio broadcasts of "News at Dictation Speed" and copying it, then making enough copies for all to read. During the day gas masks were issued. An afternoon call from regiment informed us that the enemy had capabilities in our sector to attack at any time with two panzer (armored) divisions and three infantry divisions. The day was made significant by the issuance of gas masks throughout the division. In the evening one of the guards picked up a civilian for showing a light. Captain Purington seemed to think that he could speak better French if he shouted at the man. Later, after we released the civilian, he came back to the CP with an uniformed French Army officer who could speak English. The officer explained that the civilian was a counter intelligence officer, and that the civilian, whom he knew, was a prize intelligence agent for the French, a decorated veteran of the last war, etc. That evening my birthday party consisted of several cans of sardines, crackers, etc., in the CP with other officers.

On Sunday the thirtieth, Sergeant Lester Wardell[24] initiated the use of headphones on the CP telephone to monitor telephone calls and to record them for the unit journal. That day also saw the bombing of regimental HQ in Bining; it was not clear whether it was by friendly planes or by Germans flying captured planes. It started to snow during the day.

On the thirty-first we had another alert to the possibility that the enemy would attack at any time. Friendly French troops were seen in the area on various missions

27

of reconnaissance. Later in the day intelligence channels announced that one hundred fifty enemy tanks detrained the day before in Zweibrucken. We were ordered to check all unoccupied pillboxes in our area. At this time my section consisted of Sergeant Chany, Tech 4 Bowler, Tech 5 O'Rourke, and Privates First Class Coggins and Von Hegel, with Private First Class Cortellino still with the section. There was more snow during the day. A company commander's meeting was held in the evening, during which the discussion was our possible actions in case of an attack. At midnight Adolph Hitler[25] was supposed to speak, so we stayed up long enough for him to get off a couple of words then started to call it a night. So far it had been a very quiet and tame New Year's Eve.

At 0015 the CP guard came in to tell us that he could hear small arms fire. On calling Fox Company, we found that they heard it coming from the 71st Infantry area to our left. A call from regiment stated that the 44th Division was being attacked by four or five companies of infantry and was without artillery or armored support. By 0050 it was reported to have died down, but regiment ordered us to occupy certain of our defensive positions. Fox Company was shifted to these positions. Our sleep during the rest of the night was interrupted by the telephone, chiefly higher headquarters disseminating information. As the situation cleared in the morning, it developed that some of the enemy had gotten into Rimling but that the 3rd Battalion had cleaned them out, capturing thirty-five prisoners.

During the action an OP, manned by Fox Company in a very exposed position, was forced to withdraw, as was King Company. We heard that other regiments of the division were being driven back in their sectors. After a day of minor confusion, things quieted down in our sector.[26]

In the afternoon of the first I received instructions from the 374th FA Battalion to report to the CO of the 250th Field Artillery Battalion, which was currently supporting us. This was a light corps artillery battalion and has only one liaison officer. It was planned that, in case the 44th Division fell back, the 255th Infantry (nominally a part of the 63rd Division) would be exposed while filling the gap between the 44th and the 100th and that the 250th FA Battalion would be in direct support of the 255th Infantry.[27] I was to supplement their meager artillery liaison and forward observer parties with my section and the observer parties of Baker Battery. I took a lot of maps, Private Pine, and my jeep and started out to find the 2nd Battalion of the 255th Infantry. We met quite a few troops from the 255th, loaded down with everything they had ever been issued. I finally located the 2nd Battalion 255th CP in Etting, contacted the CO, found out his plans, and discussed an artillery plan. I went through Achen and Singling on my way back to Rohrbach, stopping in at the 250th FA Battalion CP and further sharing information. We missed chow all of the way around but did get a turkey sandwich and a piece of the 250th FA Battalion CO's fruitcake. That was our New Year's Day—others were having it much harder.

After dark on the evening of the first, the 44th Division was again attacked, and at 2215 we were notified that they had withdrawn. On the morning of the second, the 397th Infantry commander ordered one company of the 2nd Battalion into position and the remaining one alerted. I took two FO parties over to the 255th Infantry and walked over the ground in their sector, improving on my previous fire plan, and submitted it to the 2nd Battalion 255th Infantry and the 250th FA Battalion. The rest of the day I was telling the 2nd Battalion 397th Infantry what rookies I thought the 63rd Division infantry were and relating all of the things I had seen them doing. I felt our division was lucky to have entered combat when the situation was on the offensive.[28]

About noon of 2 January, the 3rd Battalion was hit and the 2nd Battalion was alerted for counter-attack. George Company did counter-attack Hill 375 and took their objective. The remainder of the battalion occupied various prepared positions in our area. That afternoon saw quite a bit of activity by the rest of the 397th Infantry. We were now getting much information on the effect of the German offensive on the 100th Division and its neighbors.[29]

The early morning of the third found us getting shelled in Rohrbach. Some timid souls went to the basement, but I stayed in the CP for the rest of the hours of darkness. During this time both Easy and Fox Companies were moved around to other positions to protect our left flank after hearing that Gros Rederching has fallen into German hands. At 0730 the George Company platoon led by First Lieutenant Adolph A. Belser[30] was forced to withdraw from Hill 375.

As we were eating breakfast, a very excited man burst in on us proclaiming that the Germans were coming. When we got him quieted down we found out that he was an AT sergeant from the 255th Infantry. He had been in Achen when the Germans broke through. He finally admitted that he had actually seen only one German tank in the town. He had not used any of his AT weapons in the town but had commandeered a two-ton truck and had left as fast as he could. We sent him back to where we knew that he would find other elements of his battalion.[31]

When the Germans had attacked, neither the 255 Infantry nor the 250th FA Battalion had called me and the Baker Battery FOs to come and help them as had been planned. Later the ground was recaptured without the help of artillery.

The 2nd Battalion was having its own activity. Easy Company shot at a German amphibious "jeep" as it approached a roadblock on their left flank. This resulted in the capture of two SS prisoners and one German vehicle.[32] The battalion used the captured vehicle for months. An order came out for all vehicles to display red panels because of all the air activity in the sector.[33]

All day the enemy on Hill 375 had been causing trouble, so the 2nd Battalion was ordered to retake and hold the hill. Two platoons of George Company were selected for the task, and a platoon of tanks were to aid them. The plans called for one platoon and the tanks to stay on the hill. Captain Newton went up to direct this operation, which was completed in the evening.

During the day elements of the 2nd French Armored Division on our left counter-attacked the town of Gros Rederching—the tank being led by a general in a jeep. By evening they were in the town. The battle had been complicated by the

EXTEND NORTHWEST

Germans' use of American tanks and uniforms. The 44th Division relieved the French on the recaptured ground, and the French went to the rear.

On the morning of the fourth, the George Company platoon was being fired on, and it took a bit of action through command channels to persuade their supporting tanks up to aid them. In the afternoon I visited Hill 375, walking over the entire area with the platoon leader. We were possible targets out in the open like that.[34] We did have a scare in our otherwise peaceful walk when we tripped an illuminating flare left there by some previous occupant.

Late in the afternoon Easy Company moved one platoon into a gap west of Rimling. Plans were made to shoot artillery-illuminating shells at certain times during the night, with all companies and their OPs alerted to be on lookout for any activity at those times.[35]

The companies on line reported that their men had wet clothes and feet and were victims of diarrhea; all of those were bad for effectiveness and morale. It would not improve when the men could not move from their foxholes during daylight hours. The continuing problem of trench foot was worsened.[36]

Early on the morning of the fifth, huge explosions shook the town of Rohrbach. The CP guard swore that the shells were landing just outside of the CP. As the shells came in at five-minute intervals, I guessed that we had one large gun shooting at us. In the morning I set out to investigate and found large shell craters, none of which were closer than five hundred yards from the CP. From the fragments that I found, it was established that the shells were from a 380mm railroad gun. Later in the morning we were alerted that we were about to get orders.

Notes

1. The German offensive in the Ardennes Forest area of Luxemberg and Belgium had started in mid-December and was still going strong at this time. The resulting military actions became known as the Battle of the Bulge but were later called the Ardennes Campaign.

2. The 2nd Battalion made the move by truck to Petit Rederching then by foot the rest of the way to Kleinmuhl.

3. Pine, Donald D., Pvt., later Pfc. and Cpl., HQ 374 FA.

4. Von Hegel, William B. Pfc., radio operator, HQ 374 FA, KIA.

5. Cortellino, Charles A. Pfc., W/T, HQ 374 FA.

6. The winter of 1944-1945 had been claimed by the natives to be the coldest winter in memory. It should be noted that the Bitche area is called the Siberia of France.

7. On return to my phone I reported the time that we had crossed the border and thus got our names in the 374th FA journal.

EXTEND NORTHWEST

8. Gluesenkamp, Lester G., Combat, *A Short Interval in the Life of a G.I. in World War II*, Alma, IL, 1994.

9. This was neither the first nor last time that the FDC questioned the FOs on their enemy sighting. While trying to avoid firing on friendly troops is a desirable motive, the discrediting of those observing the enemy and with the forward elements of the friendly units is hard to justify.

10. Posit fuses for field artillery shells were highly classified devices at the time. They were fuses that activated when in the proximity of a target or the ground rather than on contact as conventional fuses did. They were more effective than the time fuses that had been used in earlier wars. The WWI shrapnel shell used a time fuse to achieve an air burst. The fuses were adapted from anti-aircraft fuses.

11. Many homes in rural villages had manure piles in front of them. The piles were on basins with sumps in them. The manure was from the livestock kept in the barns attached to the houses. Leachings of the manure by rain and other fluid settled into the sump and were removed by a pump. The pumped fluid went into wooden casks on a small cart (called "honey carts" by the GIs), and the carts were pulled out to fields and the fluid spread for fertilizer. In modern times the barn is now a garage, and the basin area is filled in to provide parking space.

12. Stallworth, William R., Capt., CO F 397 Inf. WIA.

13. Chambliss, Preston R., 2nd Lt., B 374 FA. POW.

14. Pfc. Cortellino was a wireman/telephone operator, not a radio operator, but he was the only man I had to help me carry the SCR609 radio. I had to leave Pfc. Cooper to operate the SCR610 radio.

15. Martin, James D., 2nd Lt., F 397 Inf.

16. On the twenty-ninth another patrol of the same area had much different results. (Bowman, B. Lowery & Mosher, Paul F., *op. cit.*)

17. I do not know now what the reason was. I wish that I had put it in my original manuscript.

18. When we had moved to this sector, we had moved to unwooded rolling hills, the first time since we entered combat that we were not fighting in the heavily wooded Vosges. Movement without cover was going to be a problem for us from here on out.

19. The town is actually named Rohrbach-les-Bitche. I will use Rohrbach in this account.

20. Moseley, William H., Jr., Pfc., Orderly HQ 2 Bn. 397 Inf.

21. This set-up was a rare one for an infantry battalion headquarters, but we felt that it was the usual luxury that was enjoyed by higher headquarters and even by other branches and services that were in our rear. The town had received little combat damage, but as usual, there was no electricity and the lighting, heating, and sanitary facilities were primitive.

22. Oakman, William, 1st Lt., MAC, Med. Det., 2 Bn. 397 Inf.

EXTEND NORTHWEST

23. It is apparent that my initial manuscript was reporting repeatedly that it was cold. Actually it probably was getting colder daily as winter went on. Bonn's study had figures that show such a trend over the winter months. (Bonn, Keith E., *When the Odds Were Even,* Novato, CA, 1994.)

24. Wardell, Lester C., Sgt., HQ 2-397 Inf.

25. Hitler, Adolph, German dictator.

26. The German offensive in the Alsace-Lorrainne region that started New Year's Eve has no name in my original memoirs, nor in the unit histories that were published at the same time as the memoirs were set aside. In papers that were with the manuscript is an extract from Walter Millis's 1946 *The Last Phase.* I found that the offensive was given the code name "May 10, 1940." It was established later that it was named "NORDWIND," which is its common designation used in histories of WWII. In the case of the Battle of the Bulge, it is referred to as the Ardennes Offensive rather than the German code name "WACHT AM RHEIM."

27. The 255th Infantry was attached to the 100th Division and the 253rd Infantry of the 44th Division.

28. My comments were not warranted. I had to learn later from Bonn's study that the 63rd and the 70th Divisions in the Seventh Army at that time consisted only of their respective three infantry regiments without the usual division support. These regiments consisted mostly of raw, untrained enlisted men, and a core of officers and non-coms who had not been through the usual training cycles in the field that other divisions had.

29. To our right the weak defensive forces had been pushed back, forcing the 398th Regiment to pull south and west to protect the 397th and the 399th. As had been seen, the defenses to our left had also fallen back. Thus Rimling was a part of a salient in the enemy lines.

30. Belser, Adolph A., 1st Lt., G 397 Inf.

31. This was the first experience we had with the panic the German offensive brought to some. Later we were to find out about many other cases, some that had led to group routs.

32. By now we had learned that the attack in our sector was by a German Corps that included the 17th SS Panzer Grenadier Division. The elite combat unit was quite formidable in their black uniforms, instead of the usual German gray, and had the deathhead and the double lightening bolt SS insignia.

33. Canvas panels were provided to all combat units to display to show Air Corps planes that we were friendly. They were fluorescent pink on one side and fluorescent yellow on the other. Their display of color was change as needed to help counter possible enemy use of captured panels. When the panels were not displayed, our combat units were subject to attacks from our own planes. This was something we had practiced when training with tactical air corps outfits in the states.

34. I used a helmet with my rank painted on it when I was in the combat areas. Most officers at the front did not, since the enemy made officers priority targets, but there

were other tip-offs to officers. I usually had a map case and binoculars over my shoulders and maybe a mussette bag.

35. Perhaps the tripping of the flare reminded someone that artillery flares at night have uses.

36. This was the first time that trench foot was mentioned in my memoirs. It had been a continuing problem since the divisions had entered combat in the wet and cold of October. A related cold injury was frostbite. At times shock and combat exhaustion also took their toll.

CHAPTER 4

Defend at Rimling

By 5 January 1945, the Allied forces had stopped most of the German offenses in both the Ardennes and the Lorraine sectors. New German offensive operations were started against the Seventh Army in Alsace. One area in which the German offensive had not penetrated was where the 100th Division's 397th Infantry had held around the small town of Rimling, which the Germans continued to attack. The author accompanied the 2nd Battalion, 397th Infantry, which relieved the 3rd Battalion during the night of the fifth. The enemy infantry and armor still tried to take the town from the northwest. The 2nd Battalion resisted daylight and night attacks through the eighth; however, on the morning of the ninth it had lost control of part of the town and one of its companies had been captured. The 2nd Battalion and its attachments were ordered to move out of the town during the night of January ninth.

On 5 January, at 1000, the 2nd Battalion, 397th Infantry was ordered to relieve the 3rd Battalion in Rimling. The 2nd Battalion's Easy Company was already on the line to the left of Rimling. The 3rd Battalion's Love Company, which had not borne much fighting, would remain on the line to the right of town. Major Wisdom and Captain McAllister went to the 3rd Battalion CP in Rimling at 1300, and I joined them later. Our route was the road into the town along the skyline, over Hill 370, and was obviously under observation by the enemy since any movement on it drew artillery fire. It was a cold, clear day and visibility was excellent, which necessitated a speedy trip, but the road downhill with curves, shell craters, and a lot of snow and ice. It was a choice; either go slow and risk artillery fire or go fast and risk a smash-up, and Private First Class Coggins almost gave me one. On arrival I discussed the situation with First Lieutenant Robert Smith, then our liaison officer with the 3rd Battalion.[1]

The house that we came to on the fifth of January little resembled the one in which we had visited the 3rd Battalion CP on the twenty-eighth of December

DEFEND AT RIMLING

after the patrol into Erching. Both artillery shells and high velocity tank rounds battered the house. The command center had been moved from the ground floor to a long, low potato cellar. This cellar had a crawl space up into the house proper, a small window out to the rear, and a blanket-covered doorway on the street via several steps. Heat was provided by an army tent stove fed by wood, but the next evening it was replaced by a gasoline stove brought up from the rear. Light was by candles, day and night.[2]

To the rear of the CP were two artillery jeeps—one completely destroyed by mortar fire and one damaged sufficiently to require repair before it could be moved.[3] We had brought up both of our section jeeps but not the trailer. The section now consisted of Sergeant Chany, Tech 4 Bowler, Tech 5 O'Rourke, Private First Class Coggins, and Private Pine.[4] The next day I sent Chany and Coggins back for mail, radio calls, and the current authenticator code, but they did not return to Rimling.[5]

The relief of the 3rd Battalion was completed by the evening of the fifth under cover of darkness. At 2100 the 2nd Battalion assumed control. Lieutenant Smith and his section stayed overnight to acquaint us with the fire plans and wire network that they were turning over to us and to ensure complete artillery support during the change over. I went to sleep early and slept the entire night very soundly, missing the call for a normal barrage that was reported to have stopped at least a company of Germans attacking the town.

Lieutenant Smith and his section left us on the sixth. It was relatively quiet during the day, with cloudy and cold weather. We got several calls from various OPs reporting noises from Guiderkirch. Around noon we received word of an anticipated attack, based on observations of a concentration of enemy troops. There was an infiltrated sniper somewhere in the south end of town, making everyone jumpy but not doing other damage.[6] On the left of the sector, Easy Company repulsed a daylight patrol.[7]

In the evening a hot meal arrived along with a supply of sufficient K rations to last us a while in case it should not be possible to get hot food to us at some future time. Papers that came up with the chow included orders promoting Major Wisdom to lieutenant colonel and also a 100th Division situation map. Major Wisdom was promoted under very informal and dismal surroundings. The situation map showed the division was out on a limb with adjacent units on both sides as well as to our rear. After a quick look at the map we burned it—that was the sort of document that we could not risk falling into enemy hands. First Lieutenants Thomas Busbee[8] and Joe Mounsey[9] came to the CP to tell of the poor shape of their troops on the heights west of the town. Their units, elements of Fox and George Companies, had been dug in, exposed to raw winter weather on expanses of open terrain longer than the troops in the protection of houses. The lieutenants asked that their units be relieved. They had to depart with a promise of relief when it was possible, but all of the troops under the command of the 2nd Battalion were on line.

At 2200 we sent out the order for all companies to report by telephone every

DEFEND AT RIMLING

half hour. These contacts and their conversations helped to relieve a lot of the tension all the way around. From this time on Colonel Wisdom, Captain McAllister, and I rotated, having an officer on duty at all times and letting the two off duty get some rest. I was already rotating with my men on our artillery radio, as only two of the three could operate it. I finally went to sleep at 0100 on the morning of the seventh, Sunday, after writing several personal letters, one to my younger brother still in high school.

At 0330 I was being shaken awake. Rimling had just received a terrific barrage of mortars, rockets, artillery, and tank fire. This noise had aroused everyone but me. The firing had knocked out most of the telephone lines. After a minute or so of deep quiet, we heard the firefights starting. Expecting capture, we burned all the papers in the CP, including Colonel Wisdom's promotion orders and my freshly written letters home. We heard several nearby explosions that we were told were caused by German tanks firing at what they took to be strong points. From our cellar it was hard to tell from which direction the sounds of firing were coming.

Everyone became an observer for artillery fire, and I was busy keeping several fire missions straight at once. A communication network of telephones, artillery radios, and infantry radios handled fire missions.

We started a period in which we wished for daylight when it was night and wished for darkness when it finally was light. Calls from the rear asking for information interfered with our handling operations by radio. Nearness of the SCR-300 infantry radios and the artillery SCR-610 radios also caused interference. The confusion of firefights and artillery fires was preferred to the lull that followed when we didn't know who owned the ground around us. As daylight neared it was rather quiet, and we were wishing that we had all of the noise of a couple of hours earlier. All available men in the CP group, including the men in our section, were posted upstairs in our building for local defense, whatever their armament. I had difficulties with my radio communications with the 374th FA Battalion Fire Direction Center; they challenged me for authentication, which I could not give. We had burned our one authentication code when we had burned our other papers.[10] It was cold and foggy, and visibility was poor.

Then we had our tense situation with a German tank. We heard the noise of a tank motor approaching. We knew that there were no friendly tanks in the village. The tank got closer. A voice relay from our guards above told us that a German tank was approaching along the street, and they reported that it had German infantry on it. It was quiet (German tanks made one-tenth the noise of the American tanks). Soon the tank was in front of the CP, which was the only building on that street that had a multitude of footprints in the snow and many telephone wires converging on the door opening covered by OD blankets. The tank stopped, the guards told us, but we knew because we could hear the tread clanking stop. The candles were extinguished. Everyone flattened against the wall and held his breath, only to be more aware of the murmur of the tank motor. We could imagine the

DEFEND AT RIMLING

turret of the tank turret turning toward our entrance and a shell smashing through the blanket curtained door into our small room.

A plea went up to the guards in the house above us to fire a bazooka at the tank. The men were trying to fire one, but they were unfamiliar with the safety mechanism on the new model of bazooka. Before we could get instructions to them, we heard a couple of pops and then the noise of the tank slowly backing up the street in the direction in which it came. The pops had been the noise of hand grenades thrown by an alert infantryman—the grenades had wounded some of the German infantry riding on the tank and caused the tank to withdraw. In the daylight we found one German killed by the grenades, but others must have been wounded and evacuated.[11]

In the morning we found that all of our positions west and north of the town of Rimling had been driven in, and the Germans held some buildings in the town. All of the battalion AT guns were out of order. I found Lieutenant Devereaux, who had been FO with George Company on Hill 375, casually firing artillery missions for Easy Company: when the troops from George Company had withdrawn to Guising, he had moved to the lines west of Rimling. It was snowing, which limited the visibility.

The units in town were ordered to clear the houses occupied by the Germans. A major part of the clearing of the village was accomplished by Technical Sergeant Charles Carey[12] and the men of AT platoon. He and some of his men brought their prisoners to the battalion CP for interrogation and evacuation to the rear. In addition to all of the equipment of a combat infantryman, Sergeant Carey was loaded down with several German pistols that he had taken from prisoners he had captured. He offered the CP personnel their choice of the pistols. I took a Walther P-38 pistol and a Mauser 7.65 automatic.

As the prisoners were brought to the Battalion CP area, they were given a thorough search. Most of them had American cigarettes from K rations. The wounded were taken care of by a poorly equipped but efficient German enlisted medic—he was rather old, especially in comparison with the young SS troops on whom he worked.

While we were looking over the prisoners, a couple of very angry riflemen brought in a prisoner, keeping him closely covered with their M-1 rifles. It developed that he had been in a barn and surrendered to the mop-up squad, then shot and killed the first man coming to get him out. First Lieutenant Leo Rabinowitz[13] was very upset by the incident. We found out that the prisoner could speak some English. He admitted to the shooting, and when asked why, his only answer was that his leaders made him do it. He had no further excuse when it was pointed out that there were no leaders present. Very few German non-coms and none of their officers were captured that day.

The prisoners, over fifty-five SS men, were assembled in front of a light machine gun in front of the CP and later taken to the rear by a defiladed route.[14] That

DEFEND AT RIMLING

night we found out that volumes of information had been obtained while interrogating the group but that it could not be sent up to us. We did think that this group of prisoners helped the higher headquarters to get a better picture of the situation at Rimling.

Later in the day I accompanied Colonel Wisdom, by a circuitous route, to the Fox Company CP. On the way we passed a burning disabled tank with all of the crew members, except one, dead on the ground. That crew member had been part way out of the turret when he was seriously injured, and he could not move from a sure death by fire. His pleas and motions for aid were ignored.

At the Fox Company CP more prisoners were being collected. In the snow around the CP were the remains of several American soldiers, most of them killed by the fire from the tanks that had been in town.[15] The company commander's jeep in front of the CP had been rather thoroughly demolished by one tank round. Another tank round had been put through the CP door. It was reported that Second Lieutenant Frank Rosse[16] was missing, and it was thought he had been killed.

During the day two German tanks had come into town from the west. We were told that Tech Sergeant Carey had disabled one with a bazooka and burned the other, killing the crew by rifle fire as they left the tank; this was probably the burning tank we had seen. The Germans evacuated both tanks during the following night.[17]

On returning to the CP we resumed our requests to the rear for TDs to be sent up to us since our AT guns were out of service. Plans were made to deploy our remaining forces over the territory we still held. Fox Company held the north and west edge of town. Easy Company held the southwest, the direction of our rear, as we had no contact in that direction. Easy Company sent patrols on schedule during the hours of darkness to contact elements to the rear.

In the afternoon two TDs were sent up from Bettviller, but one got stuck in crossing the creek. The other, guided by Sergeant Carey, was put in a position in the south part of town. On the next day that TD managed to knockout or turn back tanks trying to cut off the town from the west. Before dark the company commander of King Company came up and announced that his company was to join us. His unit and its attached Mike Company support were designated battalion reserve and were ordered to occupy centrally located houses in the town. The FO assigned to this company was First Lieutenant Henry Jackson,[18] and he was a welcomed addition to our supply of FOs; the more eyes and communications for the artillery the better.

In the evening I had a big surprise when the switchboard called us and announced that we had a wire routing to the rear through a 3rd Battalion wire. I discussed our situation with Captain Newton, and arrangements were made to pick up badly needed supplies, especially radio batteries, at the creek east of town. The plan did not work out that way, however, and the How Company mortar platoon got most of the supplies; they did not need them as badly as other units in the battalion did.[19] The wire contact did not stay in very long.

Fairly early on the night of 8 January the enemy hit us with tanks and infantry.

DEFEND AT RIMLING

Captain Stallworth, at the CP for instructions, sat down and soon was asleep and forgotten. Fox Company had been hit, and we could not establish radio contact with them. From telephone conversations with the How Company CP, located near Fox Company, we got enough information to convince us that Fox Company had been overrun. While we were discussing it we suddenly discovered that the Germans had not captured the company commander; he was asleep with us in the CP. Most of Fox Company, including Lieutenants Rabinowitz,[20] Martin, Saxton,[21] and Nay[22] were missing. Lieutenant Chambliss was also missing[23] with his FO party. The remainder of the FO party consisted of Private First Class Grady Brown,[24] Private First Class Frank Skokan,[25] and Private Carl Peterson.[26]

In the morning the loss of Fox Company was verified, and the Germans again occupied that part of Rimling. The situation was such that Lieutenant Colonel Wisdom decided not to try to clear out the town as on the previous day. We were concerned that the enemy might try to clear us out, and so all of our souvenirs of the previous day were hidden in the potatoes so that we would not be found possessing them if captured. It was tempting to try an offensive move to recapture the Fox Company men, but there was considerable evidence that the Germans had evacuated the prisoners under the cover of darkness.

During my period as duty officer at the 2nd Battalion CP I answered the few calls that we had on the remaining telephone lines. I had two conversations with Sergeant Carey in which he urged that the battalion should attempt to recapture our men and clear the Germans out of town. At last he told me that he was taking some of his men in an attempt to find one of his non-coms who had been left in a building the previous evening. A while later two of his men came back with tears in their eyes. It was reported that a sniper bullet to the head killed Sergeant Carey. He was awarded the Congressional Medal of Honor posthumously for his deeds in Rimling. They were the most outstanding deeds of aggressive soldiering that I have ever been near.

We found out later that Lieutenant Bradshaw's mortar platoon of How Company had an action of its own that day. A company of German infantry, supported by tanks, tried to attack from the west to the east, south of town, to cut us off. The tanks were knocked out or turned back by the TD, as mentioned previously. The SS infantry ran into the mortar platoon, which fought with mortars, carbines, and pistols. When it was over the mortar platoon had no casualties, and it had either killed or captured the entire company, as verified by the records of the German first sergeant.[27]

That day movement was at a minimum because of sniper fire. The 2nd Battalion HQ Company group protecting the CP had a firefight with King Company, with no damage done. We received word of a counter-attack to be made from Guising over the well-fought-over Hill 375 to join up with our west flank and restore lost ground. It was to be the 1st Battalion, 398th Infantry, supported by tanks and TDs. We felt that we could aid it by artillery fire, as some observers were in good positions to see the enemy operating against the effort. When a message

DEFEND AT RIMLING

was decoded that they had reached elements of our forces, tears came to our eyes, but a check showed the decoding to be faulty. It stated that our artillery was falling on friendly troops. (So much for using observers who were not with the troops being supported.) The counter attacked ceased. We had several reports during the operation of what one observer reported as "two of the biggest tanks I have ever seen." These were later proven to be Panzer Jager tanks.[28]

Spirits were low in Rimling as darkness fell. It had been our first day of strictly passive defense, without the earlier clearing out the town. We felt that the counter attack had failed.[29] Rumors were heard that the enemy was to attack to our rear after dark in an attempt to cut us off. Our sole TD was nearly out of ammunition and could not move, as its starting battery was dead. Worst of all was the common knowledge that our orders were to hold at all costs. We were starting to realize what "at all costs" meant. A few of us knew of the message that Lieutenant Colonel Wisdom had sent out, saying that we could not hold much longer.

We received word by radio to stand by for orders. These were not long in coming, by means of the intelligence sergeant of the 3rd Battalion. We were to withdraw, crossing the stream to the east of Rimling and going to Guising by way of Bettviller. Artillery was to furnish a screen of close fires south and west of town. Tanks were to meet us at the creek and act as a rear guard. Movement started at once. I quickly arranged for Lieutenant Colonel Wisdom a plan for the artillery screening fires after our departure and stayed behind to encode the plan and get it out by radio. It seemed like using the pre-arranged code took forever. He had also ordered me to have all possible fire placed on the town at a time when we were sure that all were withdrawn. I planned to give word to start firing when I reached the first telephone after leaving town. We thought about any Fox Company men who might be isolated but not captured, but we had no evidence that there were any.

My section and I loaded our jeep to capacity, leaving behind that for which we had no room. We didn't know whether the radio jeep battery would turn over the engine until we tried to start up but did not want to make the starter noise until we were ready to get on out of there.[30] It did start, and we took off with Private Pine as the driver. At the edge of town we caught up with the last of the foot troops, which slowed us down. Driving was difficult in the dark and snow over the shell-marked road. The screening barrages were falling close. One round was within twenty-five yards of us, and Pine jumped out, letting the jeep run into the ditch. I got Pine up and convinced him that the fire was friendly, as we all pushed the jeep out of the ditch.[31] We crossed the creek and started to catch up with the other jeeps from the battalion, which were having trouble of their own. The ground from the creek to the road was cut up by the treads of tracked vehicles, then frozen and covered over with snow. Private Pine drove past several jeeps that were stuck, and then he took us off of the beaten path, going through a fence and dodging other obstacles. While it was dark with complete blackout, some dark objects showed up against the white snow. We were busy keeping our equipment and ourselves from being tossed from the bouncing jeep—we might have lost a few things. Some jeeps and trailers were abandoned, but not ours.

When we again got on the road, we went to Bettviller, where I found the 1st Battalion CP and Lieutenant McGuire. Using his phone I called the 374th FA Battalion Fire Direction Center and talked to Major Green. It took some talking to convince him that Lieutenant Colonel Wisdom had ordered all possible artillery fire be placed on Rimling and that the town was clear of friendly troops. The fire was delivered, but one error was made when a reinforcing French battalion used white phosphorous shells; this, of course, illuminated the area and might have exposed our troops moving on the road, but no German fire was drawn.

We did not locate the road to Guising and so went by way of Petit Rederching and Rohrbach. By now we were quite cold from our jeep ride. I knew where the 3rd Battalion was in Rohrbach and went there to warm up. It turned out that it was now their rear CP, but they informed us that the 2nd had reached Guising. We gratefully received our first hot food in a few days. We then went up to the 3rd Battalion forward CP where, with Lieutenant Smith, I found the FO parties that had been in Rimling. We inventoried for the MIA and WIA—only Lieutenant Chambliss and his party were missing. I phoned that information to the 374th FA Battalion CP then got the FO parties with their normal companies.[32] I then went to Rohrbach and let my adrenalin run out.[33] By 2300 I turned in for some much needed sleep.[34]

Notes

1. This had not been a battalion-for-battalion relief. Fox Company relieved King Company. George Company continued to try to hold Hill 375 southwest of town. How Company relieved Mike Company with its various weapons locations on the north edge of town and its mortar platoon in the draw south east of town. The 2nd Battalion HQ Company relieved the 3rd Battalion HQ Company elements in and about Rimling. As noted, Love Company remained on line to the east of Rimling, and Easy Company was already on line west and south of Rimling. In the change no Baker Battery FO manned the church steeple where Charlie Battery FO, Second Lieutenant James S. Howard, had performed the deeds that earned him the Distinguished Service Cross.

2. The house, which had been pretty well shot up in 1945, was completely restored when I visited in May of 1998. It is located at 47 Grand Rue. The crawl space up into the house is now closed. The potato cellar is still there and is being used to store potatoes; the ledges along either side that had several layers of potatoes on which we had sat in mid-winter had only a few small potatoes scattered on them in May. The occupant of the house in 1998 was a man who was seventy-eight years old, who claimed that he had been in the house during the early days of 1945. He would have been of military age in the period 1940-1944 and subject to military service with either the French or German armies. Neither Charles Cortellino, who had been in the house with

DEFEND AT RIMLING

the 3rd Battalion CP, nor I, who was there with the 2nd could believe him—he must have had a good hiding place. The citizens of Rimling suffered by not having had a chance to get out of town. Usually Civil Affairs personnel take residents to the rear when there is to be fighting in a town, but this had not been possible in the case of Rimling. Civilians had to share the cellars of houses with soldiers, and many were killed or wounded in the fighting.

3. Normally, damaged vehicles would be repaired or evacuated at night by vehicle maintenance personnel and equipment. In this situation evacuation of injured personnel was very difficult, and normal evacuation of the dead or vehicles was not even attempted.

4. Private First Class Cortellino, who had been excess in my section on New Year's Eve had gone to Lieutenant Smith's section and had been with them through the first five days of the Rimling defense.

5. This left us with the radio equipped jeep in town, and we had little use for the wire jeep taken back by Chany and Coggins, but we could have used the authentication codes. The section did not need to daily get the password-for-the-day; that we could get from the infantry.

6. We knew that the enemy was south of us, as well as to the west and north, but our habitual thinking made us consider our front to be to the north, as our rear elements were to the south. Having a sniper to the south just seemed to be having him to the rear. Actually our front was to the northwest and in the town our rear was the southeast.

7. Angier, John C. III, *A 4F R-er Goes to War with the 100th Division*, Bennington, VT, (1999).

8. Busbee, Thomas I., 1st Lt., G 397 Inf.

9. Mounsey, Joe F., 1st Lt., F 397 Inf. POW.

10. The authentication system utilized by the 374th FA Battalion was a system of two letter code groups used in firing missions. It was changed daily. We did not get the last daily change, so we could not prove who we were. By my sending Major Greene a message based on the names of his and my wives, I was able to get a code group that set my authentication system right.

11. After it was all over, we realized that the bazooka not firing was probably for the best. If fired it might have caused the infantry accompanying the tank to seek the cause of the event and resulted in the killing or capture of those in the vicinity or the resulting fire and explosion of the tank's contents would have wiped a few of us out.

12. Carey, Charles F. Jr., T/Sgt., AT Plat. HQ 2 397 KIA.

13. Rabinowitz, Leo, 1st Lt., F 397 KIA.

14. I did not believe that the prisoner who had shot our man got to the rear, but I did not write that into my original text.

15. In the situation that we were in, it was not reasonable to collect the dead and evacuate their bodies to the rear for graves registration processing.

DEFEND AT RIMLING

16. Rosse, Frank J., 2nd Lt., 2 397 KIA.

17. The Germans evacuated their dead and reclaimed disabled vehicles at night. We did not and couldn't even get a battery for a TD during darkness. The night captures of our men by the Germans in December had shown us how adept the Germans were at operations at night.

18. Jackson, Henry G., 1st Lt., FO C 374 FA.

19. By now our units were not in close contact with each other, and the sending of runners to get the supplies from the How Company mortar platoon was not implemented. It is significant that the defiladed route to the rear had been defined and that the exposed route used for a week did not have to be the only route to and from Rimling.

20. Those captured with Lieutenant Rabinowitz reported that he had been segregated from the officer prisoners and lead away. His body was eventually buried in the Lorraine (St. Avold) American Cemetery under the Star of David. He may have been sorted out and identified because of his dog tags.

Identification tags were widely known as dog tags. Two identical tags were worn by all uniformed personnel. They were the sole item of identification issued. The tags were thin metal and had the person's identification pressed into them. They were hung on two beaded metal chains. One chain was long enough to go over the head; it had one tag on it, and the small chain of the second tag. In the event of the person's death, the tag on the small chain was removed and sent through military channels as proof of death. The large chain stayed with the remains until burial, when the other tag was removed and attached to the grave marker.

The tags bore the name and serial number of the person. Symbols indicated blood type, date of the latest tetanus shot, and religious preference. In 1942 they also showed the full address to be notified in case of death. As the war progressed the metal in the tags was changed and the address eliminated to prevent that information from being used for propaganda purposes by the Nazis. Unfortunately the religious preference of C, P, or H was not eliminated and lead to the execution of many Jews captured by the Germans.

21. Saxton, Rayford E., 1st Lt., F 397 POW.

22. Nay, Robert E., 2nd Lt., F 397 POW.

23. It was reported that Lieutenant Chambliss called the Baker Battery CO on the telephone and discussed surrendering with him. Why he did not at least call to me or someone in the 2nd Battalion CP is not known; he left us thinking that Fox Company had an artillery observer when they did not have one. (Fishpaw, Eli and Fishpaw, Bernice, *op. cit.*)

24. Brown, Grady H., Pfc., FO Party, B 374 FA POW.

25. Skokan, Frank M., Pfc., FO Party, B 374 FA POW.

26. Peterson, Carl A., Pvt., FA Party, B 374 FA POW.

27. This platoon action, plus other actions by How Company members in Rimling, earned that company the Distinguished Unit Citation. The 3rd Battalion also received a Distinguished Unit Citation for their defense of Rimling.

28. That is what my manuscript says. I think that there was an error. The Germans attacking us were equipped with both Mark V Panther and Mark VI Tiger tank (75mm and 88mm guns, respectively). They also had attached to them one of the only two German battalions of Jager Tiger tank destroyers (with 128mm guns), the largest tracked vehicles in the Wehrmacht. The latter may have been the large tanks reported.

29. The effort by the 398th at Rimling had achieved their objective of relieving the pressure on the Rimling defenders.

30. Usually vehicles equipped with radios or other devices that operated off of the vehicle battery were run daily to recharge their batteries. On this day we had not tried to operate our jeep to prevent calling attention to our presence. Our battery was not as low as we thought it might be.

31. Our withdrawal that night did not end the story of our defense of Rimling. As will be seen, over the next two months relevant finding were made.

32. Having two Baker Battery jeeps to transport three FO parties led to confusion when all three rifle companies moved at the same time.

33. Having the responsibilities of both getting artillery fire on Rimling and getting my frightened section personnel back to where they felt safe had kept my mind off of personal concerns. When it was all over I had an emotional letdown.

34. Earlier my memoirs were repeating the mention of the cold weather. In the past two chapters the mention of getting sleep is often repeated. The cold weather had continued, but I must have become acclimated to it.

CHAPTER 5

Shifts

By 10 January 1945, the German attacks in the Lorraine sector of the Seventh Army had ceased as the German efforts were directed towards Alsace. The 100th Division made some adjustments in their front lines and moved the sectors of its regiments. When the 1st Battalion, 398th Infantry took over the Rimling sector on 11 January, the author continued to stay with the sector and the 1st Battalion, 398th Infantry until the 44th Division, in turn, took over that sector on 18 January. The 397th Infantry moved to positions to the east of the 44th Division. The author rejoined the 2nd Battalion, 397th Infantry with its headquarters at Frohmuhl as it settled into a small sector for the winter. By the end of January the shifting fronts and sectors were complete in the XV Corps, but military actions in other parts of the Seventh Army were still continuing. The period saw several shifts in personnel.

On 10 January I visited the CP of the 374th FA Battalion with the three men of my sections who had been in Rimling. While we were there Brigadier General John B. Murphy[1] visited also.[2] I picked up Sergeant Chany and Private First Class Coggins with our other jeep and returned to the 2nd Battalion 397 CP at Rohrbach. We tried to relax and get our equipment and ourselves into shape that afternoon.

In the evening a jeep raced through town, dropping two unfamiliar types of land mines in the road. We immediately thought of the alert that we had received about German agents behind our lines in our uniforms who were causing disruptions by such action. It was discovered, however that some engineer jeep had dropped two British mines, which the Americans had started to use. So ended our only scare of the day. Quite a change from preceding days!

Reorganization of the 2nd Battalion started on the eleventh. Lieutenant Heitman was placed in command of George Company. Lieutenant Mounsey joined Captain Stallworth in the reorganization of what was left of Fox Company. Orders came for a rotation of dispositions. The 397th Infantry was to move to the right, and the

SHIFTS

398th Infantry were to take over their sector, with the 2nd Battalion, 397th Infantry as the regimental reserve for the 398th Infantry. The direct support field artillery battalions (374th and 375th FA Battalions) were not to change sectors but were to continue in their present positions. Soon after I received instructions to turn over my liaison duties with the 2nd Battalion 397th to the liaison officer from the 250th FA Battalion—he was to be LnO-2 for the 374th FA Battalion, and I was to be the 374th FA Battalion's LnO-4 with the 1st Battalion, 398th Infantry.

I protested, claiming the 2nd Battalion, 397th Infantry, knew me and my section and that the 250th FA Battalion liaison officer could just as well serve with the 1st Battalion, 398. Actually I wanted my men and myself to get more rest before we moved into a new situation, but the original instructions were not changed.

As I was getting ready to move the section, I happened to be in the CP of the 2nd Battalion, 397th Infantry when a call came in for Lieutenant Colonel Wisdom. As the only officer present, I took the call and heard Major General Withers A. Burress[3] on the other end.[4] We had a short chat on the Rimling action with some emphasis on the artillery aspects of it. The conversation ended with orders for Lieutenant Colonel Wisdom to call Freedom 6 when he came back to the CP.

I located the rear CP of the 1st Battalion, 398th Infantry and met Major Ralph C. McCrumb,[5] then acting as executive officer, and then was taken up to the forward CP in Guising, where I met Major Dorris B. Odell,[6] who was acting as the commanding officer. They had the sector north of Guising facing Hill 375, which had given George Company so much trouble during the first week of January. Their company positions were in the ones that the 2nd Battalion, 397th Infantry had prepared while in reserve from 28 December to 4 January.

The next few days lose their identity in my memory. One activity was improvement of the defensive positions, such as laying barbed wire and mines. Another activity of the battalion was patrolling. I found myself a key figure in the patrol planning as I had been over almost every foot of ground in front of the battalion sector. This battalion sent one of the intelligence section men of HQ Company on every patrol, with the mission of only observing, but the patrols did not bring back much information. One man was shot when a patrol tried to come in to the lines in another battalion's sector. The study of men being questioned on their return from patrol was an interesting lesson in psychology.

This battalion was the one that had made the counterattack south of Rimling on 7 January. Several attempts were made, under the cover of darkness, to recover the bodies of the casualties of that action, but no bodies were located due to the deep snow. Some of these bodies were recovered as late as two month later, when the snow had melted.

Most of the Able Company of this battalion had been captured in Wingen on 4 December.[7] The company was reconstituted by using officers and men from the rest of the battalion along with raw replacements. My observations lead to a conclusion that the company was still not up to par with the two other rifle companies of the battalion.

SHIFTS

I can remember that I worked with Captain Edmund L. Rundell[8] and First Lieutenant Kenneth Jones,[9] but I do not remember the others. It was the only time I was with an infantry battalion headquarters that I did not sleep in the CP. Every night after the staff work was over, I went through the snow and dark to a nearby building where I slept with the artillery radio and switchboard. During this period Pine was made Private First Class, and Private First Class Coggins left the section to be replaced by Private Warren G. Southard.[10] I missed having Coggins in the section, and I felt that Southard was never as effective as Coggins had been.

The Civil Affairs personnel evacuated those civilians who wanted to get away from the fighting area. Some always stayed, however, to protect their property and livestock. Because the Germans carried on spying and sabotage by sending persons through the lines as civilians, there were strict curfew and movement restrictions. One boy, about eight or ten years old, was picked up in Bettviller when he was seen to tie a sack to a dog and turn the dog loose. The sack was recovered, and it and the boy were brought to Guising from nearby Bettviller. The sack contained a small pack of cigarettes and a death announcement, the latter printed in German, the language of the sector. The boy's story was that he was sending it to his grandfather, who lived in Guising. The grandfather was found and the boy's story accepted—they were both sent on their way after a stiff warning. No one ever did try to determine which way the dog was trained to go, but there was some talk of killing all dogs in the sector to prevent them from being used as message carriers through the lines.

At 1000 one morning in January we heard some screaming sounds followed by three loud explosions in nearby Bettviller. Then there were more screams and three explosions in our vicinity in Guising. They were the first "screaming meemies" that I recognized on hearing them.[11] Lieutenant Jones called from the infantry switchboard and said that something had landed near their building. I set out in that direction and started to look for craters. After wading through a lot of snow, I finally found three craters in an orchard in almost the opposite direction from the CP from Jones's switchboard. I examined the craters, taking measurements, looking for casing fragments, and seeking for other possible information. The craters were about ten feet in diameter and six feet in depth in the frozen ground. I found chunks of frozen dirt as big as cubes one foot on edge—thrown several yards from a crater. The heat of the explosions had melted the snow some distance around each crater.

I was thinking about what powerful things these rockets were as I walked away from the craters. Then I heard more screamings! Not being near enough to any crater to jump into, I flung myself into the snow on the frozen ground. The incoming rounds hit at short intervals, with enough time between them for me to believe that the next one would hit me. I saw the snow kicked up by flying fragments inside the limited range of my vision as I lay with my face to the ground. After six explosions I heard no more screams coming and cautiously got up.[12] In a nice circle around me I saw six fresh craters, none more than fifty yards from me. Fortunately

SHIFTS

the rockets had a lot of explosive and not too much metal in the casings. They had a lot of blast effect but not as many fragments as an artillery shell. I grabbed a couple of very hot casing fragments and hurried back to the CP. Luckily I had leather outer gloves on, as the fragments were still hot enough to char the wooden table on which I laid them. In calling in the shelling report for the event, I told the S-2 that I was done examining shell craters, and I sincerely meant it at the time. It was a couple of days before I would wander far from any protective building.

My encounter with the rockets aroused my interest in them, and I sought information on them. I found that the ones I had experienced were 210mm Neblewerfers.[13] By the time I was able to see unfired rockets and their launchers, I was well informed on them. This search led to a study of artillery shell reports, in which I hadn't been well trained. I acquired knowledge of crater and fragment analysis that was very helpful in my duties as an artillery liaison officer.[14] During the next several weeks that were in a static situation, this often was put to practice.

I was asked to undertake an unusual task by the CP personnel of the 374th FA Battalion: find a German gas mask canister for them. It was obviously a difficult task to find a discarded one in the snow. I finally got one from a prisoner. At least I knew what it was for—I had demonstrated a practical use for it in October when we were in the base camp after disembarking.[15]

On 18 January the boundaries were changed. A battalion of the 44th Division was to relieve the 1st Battalion, 398th Infantry and the 397th Infantry was to relieve the rest of the 398th Infantry. The relief was completed under the cover of darkness. For a while I was the senior officer in the sector as all of the relieved unit staff left before the relieving unit staff arrived. As usual the artillery supporting the departing unit supported the arriving unit overnight.

On the morning of 19 January, I went back to the 374th FA Battalion CP with my section. There we met the other two liaison sections, one of the few times that the three sections were together in combat. The 374th FA Battalion was back again to its usual role of supporting the 397th Infantry. We were soon on our way to find the 2nd Battalion. I found their rear CP in Petit Rederching and was told that the forward CP was being established in Frohmuhl. Going to Frohmuhl I found that the location was little more than a named road junction.[16] I found a house for my section and proceeded to the CP.

The CP at Frohmuhl was in a small three-room house. It was so small that personnel from the rear CP never came up to join us, even though we felt like we were a rear echelon installation ourselves. The 2nd Battalion had a sector large enough for a full strength company, but it had to use more than one company to man it until the rifle company's strengths were restored to a more reasonable size.

Settling down for an indefinite period was a gradual process; we did not know when we might have to move. As luck would have it, this was one of the poorest CPs that the 2nd Battalion had ever had, and we stayed here the longest. For the first time we ran into the problem of fuel for heat. Most of the civilians had been

SHIFTS

set for the winter, but those in Fromuhl seemed to be lacking. The only source of heat in the CP building was a cook stove. A conventional room heater was brought in, and the cook stove became a piece of furniture in the corner. The CP operations personnel had a gasoline tent stove in their room, simplifying their fuel supply, but the command post personnel had our fuel problems. It took a bit of jeep travel and requisitioning to get our fuel—coal. Lieutenant Colonel Wisdom fell into a snow covered hole while guiding the engineers and wrenched his back; we imported an overstuffed chair for him, our only luxury.

The evenings were long. Our lighting consisted of a jeep battery powered light, or, if the Colonel was using his jeep, by candles. We later tried to run line for the aid station, which now had a generator, but the wire losses were too great for the current needed for lighting. As Lieutenant Clark was staying with his communications platoon, we did not have a radio broadcast receiver in the CP.

Radio broadcasts were entertaining those in the battalion who had access to a telephone. By asking the switchboard for radio broadcast, anyone with a telephone could be plugged into a line to the radio and listen to whatever was tuned in. In the evenings almost every line into the switchboard was used to listen to this entertainment. Several times various groups in the battalion used this network to put on an hour program of music and jokes. This later entertainment was prompted by the organization and production of "home talent" shows by Chaplain Teeter.[17]

As only two hot meals were served each day most of the time we were here, we became accustomed to the 10-in-1 rations issued in lieu of the other meal. Usually this third meal was in the form of evening snacks. We also used the contents of packages from home to improvise snacks. One favorite dish was snow ice cream flavored with cocoa or other drink flavors.

Much of this region had been used as a maneuver area by both French and German troops when they used Camp de Bitche for training. Hottviller, just behind our lines, was a ghost town as a result of this action and had not been inhabited for several years. There were duds of all caliber shells and nationality lying around in the town. Very few of the houses were of any use for frontline shelter.

Supply was a problem that started when the combat units operating in the Ardennes had needed extra supplies for their operations. Our food was of poor quality for a while as depots and rail facilities had been depleted, moved, or destroyed when the German winter offensive was seen to be threatening. Gasoline was in very short supply. Artillery and mortar ammunition was rationed for quite a while because of the vast amount fired in repelling the German offensives. Our mortar men experimented and found that they could fire the 80mm German mortar rounds to aid in relieving their shortage of their issued 81mm ammunition.

At the end of January I had a three day rest from the daily 0700 awaking by the 374th FA Battalion S-2 section's telephone call asking about any previous night's activities. I went back to the 374th FA Battalion's Rest Center, with Service Battery, in the town of Saare-Union. Lieutenant Perry took over my duties while I

SHIFTS

was gone. Sergeant Chany was at the Division Rest Center in the same town at the same time. About this time Pine was promoted to corporal, and on 29 January Moynahan was commissioned a second lieutenant.[18]

The 374th FA Battalion had moved to Petit Rederching because of the change of sectors. I learned that First Lieutenant Eli J. Fishpaw[19] had become battery commander of Baker Battery. Major Robert B. Allport[20] was now the battalion commander. Major John E. Aber[21] had replaced Major Coleman as the battalion executive officer.

The 397th Infantry had a new regimental commander assigned on 25 January, Lieutenant Colonel Gordon Singles.[22]

On the first of February, Captain Newton was promoted to major. Major Cammeron[23] had joined the 2nd Battalion attached as an observer. It was a bit difficult for both him and those around him as he was in the position of an extra cog in a wheel; however, when we started to get ideas on the improvement of front-line foxholes, he took over. Soon the engineers were producing by day and installing by night the "Cammeron Fox Hole Insert"—these were a rough, box-type of prefabricated wood lining for the holes, which gave the holes a floor and helped prevent cave-ins, especially after the weather got warmer.

Currently the mission was one of defense, and for some time the 2nd Battalion, 397th Infantry, minus those elements on line, acted a regimental reserve. Thus Lieutenant Colonel Wisdom or his staff indicated alternate position for defense against any possible threat, from any possible direction, to the engineers who worked every day digging the required foxholes. I added positions for FO parties to the plans and kept the artillery support plans up-to-date for these alternate positions. I kept the FOs with the companies off the line as well as locating the Baker Battery drivers, Privates Greci and Humphreys, in convenient spots to aid in a rapid move if needed.

My section was kept busy for some time laying telephone wire to the various alternate OPs and orienting the FO parties as to the locations. We also improved our wire to the OPs in use—only one OP was used initially, but I soon put another one at the other end of the battalion front. I visited the OPs when I thought that they needed attention from their parent artillery unit.

While reconnoitering the location for the second OP, I had an occasion to visit the entrance to a Maginot Line Fortress in our sector.[24] It was much larger than other fortifications that I had seen in the sector. This one had been defended by the Germans and taken by assault in December when we had been south of Bitche. There were duds of shells of all calibers that had bounced off of the concrete. Very little damage had been done inside by any of the shelling, and the entrance had withheld against all of the weapons that our artillery and the Tactical Air Corps had used. It was still in a good state of preservation considering the long period it had been unmanned. The embrasure mounted 75mm guns were well sited for local defense. We later found that the Germans had nothing to compare with

SHIFTS

these major French fortifications. This sector of the Maginot Line had been flanked and had to surrender when the Germans had overrun France.[25]

Along our front we initially had snipers opposite us, making movement dangerous in the daytime, but as they gradually ceased to fire at us we became bolder and bolder during the day. One day it was fairly warm, with the ground covered with snow, so I did not think that it was warm enough for the bees I could hear buzzing near me. Then I heard the distant clatter of a German machine-gun, and wondered what they could be shooting at. All at once I put the buzz and clatter together and realized that I was being shot at.[26] I hurriedly got out of there.

Damaging to the morale of the rifle company personnel (five days on line, ten days off) and the artillery FOs was a large flock of sheep that seemed to own most of no-man's-land in the regimental sector.[27] The sheep would trip flares at night and cough, sounding very human—it took a good observer to tell that they were not an enemy patrol. One normal barrage, and perhaps more, were known to be called on these animals. Their casualties were fairly light, although we were glad to leave the sector in the spring when the carcasses started to stink.

The sector was quiet and thus deceptive. One day a signal corps officer came up in search of French signal equipment in the Maginot Fort system. Without consulting those occupying the sector, he drove down a road diagonal to our front. He was in plain sight of the enemy for some distance down the road and nearly reached the German lines before he was stopped and turned back by our front line outposts.

At one time the 2nd Battalion was the only unit not committed in the division and hence was the division reserve as well as regimental reserve. This resulted in preparation of several plans for counterattacks anywhere in the division sector, all in several copies.[28] It was only possible for me to make partial plans for artillery support of these plans as they were in several direct support sectors. I often speculated on the chances for success for these—the counter-attack by the 1st Battalion, 398th Infantry at Rimling was on my mind—but we never had to execute any of the plans.

About the time that we had to prepare the counter-attack plans, I had to take my section, as well as the three forward observer parties, to Kleinmuhl to temporarily act as LnO-1 and the FOs of the 1st Battalion while a relief was being made. The CP was in the same building that we had used on 22 December, with very few changes. After an unusually long time for a relief to be accomplished, it was completed, but I again had been the only control of the sector for a short while until Lieutenant McGuire with his section and FO parties relieved us. The roads in that sector had become nearly impassable since we had been there before, and we had several jeep mishaps before we were out of there with our belongings—but I missed being in a shelling with Colonel Wisdom, in which his jeep had been damaged.[29]

As the situation became static, duties of commanders increased. The ranking commander in every town became the town commander, with all the civil affairs

SHIFTS

duties to attend. Of course we had few problems in the few houses that were called Fromuhl; most of the civilians were in a very substantial CP type pillbox near the town. The HQ Company CP in the ghost town of Hottviller was almost a joke with its "Town Commander" sign above the door. The 2nd Battalion's chief civil affairs responsibility from this structure was manning roadblocks, which resulted in quite an additional effort.

After we had used the road to Petit Rederching for over a month, it was discovered that there were many German Teller Mines in the shoulders. Fortunately they were discovered before they had done any damage as we had used the road quite carelessly until that time.

As in all static situations, both sides placed minefields. The Germans made the mistake of putting at least one minefield near the crossroads we used as a checkpoint for adjusting our artillery. Every so often, while we adjusted fire, the OPs would report that some of these mines detonated. Some shell bursts resulted in chain detonations of the mines; one chain detonation was of over fifty mines, by count from an OP.

One of the greatest problems in the entire division was the number of SIW cases during this period. A man doesn't have much chance to think in the offensive, but he does while sitting in the defensive. Some discontent was also existent in the kitchens, and it took a bit of rotation of kitchen personnel with riflemen to improve our food.[30] During this period the variety of our food shifted over the full range that was available.[31]

Notes

1. Murphy, John B., BG, CG 100 Div. Arty.

2. My section and I were emotionally and physically beat. I not only did not call attention when he entered the room, I motioned the section to stay as they were and hoped that he would not notice us in our dark corner of the room. After he had spoken to the CP personnel in the other end of the room, he came back to us and we had to talk about Rimling.

3. Burress, Withers A., MG, CG 100 Div.

4. Contact with two generals in twenty-four hours! But then they hadn't bothered us during the action.

5. McCrumb, Ralph C., Major, later Lt. Col. CO, 1 Bn. 398 Inf.

6. Odell, Dorris B., Major, ExO, 1 Bn. 398 Inf.

7. See the information in Chapter 2 about Wingen-sur-Moder. Also, Norman Caldon R., *op. cit.*, and Watson, William C., *op. cit.*

8. Rundell, Edmund L., Capt. S-3, 1 Bn. 298 Inf.

SHIFTS

9. Jones, Kenneth J., 1st Lt., Commo, 1 Bn. 398 Inf.

10. Southard, Warren G., Pvt., HQ 374 FA.

11. "Screaming meemies" was the nickname given to German artillery rockets used in WWII. They were given their names because of the shrill-pitched noise they made. In WWI the name was given to German artillery shells that screamed due to loose rotating bands.

12. In no case do I find mention in my original text of the sound of an explosion. My ears were not plugged, but for some reason the only observation that I made are relative to other results of a blast—but as I aged I found that my hearing declined.

13. This was the medium caliber of the Neblewerfer weapon the Germans used. The others were 155 and 400 mm in diameter.

14. This sort of data was more artillery intelligence than the usual information found in shell reports. Shell reports are important at tactical levels and are of local application. Strategic artillery information is generated by field artillery observation battalions using special sound and flash techniques, and their findings are used by corps artillery for strategic purposes.

15. The activated charcoal in gas mask containers is quite effective in taking the amber color out of ethyl gasoline as well as lead. Thus automotive gasoline, which was issued in the ETO, became "white gas" which could be used in mantle lanterns without destroying the bright glow of the gas mantles. The 374th FA Battalion had bought mantle lanterns in the US and had brought them to France for night use in the FDC. I had picked up a discarded German mask at our disembarkment cantonment and had shown others how to filter gasoline through it. When this canister lost its absorption capability, any discarded gas masks were buried under snow. I finally got one from a prisoner.

16. Frohmuhl (also, Frohmuhle) was the crossroad for the east-west road N-62 (between Bitche and Rohrbach) and road D-35. Another road, D-85, goes to the north, following the valley of the north-flowing tributary of the Schwalb River. This combination of road junction and bridge made it an obvious artillery target on a map, but the deep valley made it difficult to shell with any plunging fire.

17. Teeter, Bonner E., Capt., Chaplain, 2 Bn. 397 Inf.

18. The commissioning of Moynahan was a battlefield commission, one of 336 granted by the 100th Division. Most of these were to replace officers lost as casualties, especially in the infantry. The ones in the 374th FA Battalion were required by the creation of new positions. Each firing battery had to provide two more forward observers and their parities than they had been staffed for. Also, one officer was provided to be a permanent aerial observer.

19. Fishpaw, Eli L., 1st Lt., ExO, later Capt., CO, B 374 FA.

20. Allport, Robert B., Major, CO 374 FA.

21. Aber, John E., Major, ExO, 374 FA.

22. Singles, Gordon, Lt. Col., CO 397th Inf.

SHIFTS

23. Cammeron, A.N., Maj., Attached, 2 Bn. 397 Inf.

24. This was an entrance to Fort Simserhof taken by the 44th Division in early December after extensive pounding by aerial bombardment, heavy artillery, and placed charges. The 100th Division had taken an entrance to a similar Fort Simserhof at the same times and in the same fashion.

25. The Maginot Line was constructed to face Germany. Their major armaments were in tunnel-connected turrets that not only could fire to he north but could also support their nearby turrets. The arms in the turrets included artillery pieces, mortars, and machine guns. Facing the north were a supply entrance and a personnel entrance. It was the supply entrance that I examined.

26. I have heard others describe the sound of bullets passing near them as being like the buzz of bees.

27. The same flock of sheep was also in front of Item Company, 397th Inf. Bowman, B. Lowery and Mosher, Paul F., *op. cit.*

28. Copying overlays at the front consisted of making tracings—there were not photocopiers then.

29. Lieutenant Colonel Wisdom's driver was injured. I made no record of his name.

30. Non-combat losses for the 100th Division have been reported as 7,425 and the battle casualties as 4,790. In the former category were trench foot, self-inflicted wound, combat fatigue, etc.

31. In WWII the US Army used five basic types of field rations; A, B, C, D, and K. The type A field ration was the same as that used in garrison mess halls in the States. It was prepared in the portable kitchens by the cooks organic to each unit.

The C-ration of WWII consisted of small cans of meat and vegetables packaged for one man per meal, with crackers, jams, powdered drinks, cereal, sugar, etc. The canned food forms were meat and beans, meat and vegetable stew, meat and spaghetti, Spam, meat and noodles, eggs and potatoes, meat and rice, pork and beans, frankfurters and beans, ham and lima beans, and chicken and vegetables. They could be eaten cold or hot, depending on conditions.

D-rations were packaged one meal to a long cardboard pocket size box. The heavily waxed box could be burned to provide heat for the food. The boxes were labeled breakfast, dinner, or supper. The breakfast box had a small can of ham and eggs, a fruit bar, crackers, dried coffee, and sugar. The dinner and supper boxes contained a can of cheese or meat, crackers, orange or lemon powder, sugar, chocolate or other sweet, and chewing gum.

Water wasn't a ration, but its delivery to the serviceman was closely related to food service and necessary for the preparations of rations. When the men went to receive hot food, they were able to fill canteens from a canvas bag provided with small taps. Individuals also carried tablets for chlorinating water not otherwise treated.

The type B field ration was called "ten-in-one," because it could serve ten men three meals in a day—two hot meals and one cold. Heating was by using small gas stoves, candles, paraffin heaters, burning food packaging, etc.

CHAPTER 6

Remain in Place

By the end of January the ETO forces had restored the territories lost during German winter offensives. The German army reduced their western front forces in order to strengthen their lines against Russia. The shifting of fronts and sectors was complete in the XV Corps, but some action was continuing in other parts of the Seventh Army front in Alsace. The 100th Infantry Division remained in place. The infantry straightened its lines, rebuilt depleted units, and restored the fitness of personnel and equipment. Local defense and patrols were front line activities. Artillery counter battery fires were improved. The author was with the 2nd Battalion, 397th Infantry at its headquarters in Frohmuhl through the period.

As the usual duties of the anti-aircraft artillery at this time were much less, ways were tried to find uses for their capabilities. One such use was to employ their searchlights to produce artificial moonlight by shining beams at clouds in order to produce general lighting that would aid night operations. In addition the AAA radar was used to scan over the front to pick up shells being fired in the sector. Most of such radar data was used to locate enemy artillery firing positions, and we would hear that "Jolly Charlie"[1] had spotted a target for counter battery fires.

The liaison section trailer was stolen one night. My men made a search for it throughout the sector, but it was not found. A two-wheeled civilian trailer was found, and through efforts of Corporal Pine it was fixed up with sides and top and then painted. There will be more on this trailer later.

During this period all of the infantry officers went on pass to the various pass centers. I started to feel like the permanent party. Captain McAllister went to the I&E school near Paris, and the I&E programs for the troops were stepped up. One of the activities inaugurated was the nightly I&E broadcast of news to each battalion by wire from regimental headquarters that was then put out on all telephones in the same manner as our regular broadcast radio service.

REMAIN IN PLACE

Patrolling was to be aggressive, so read all of the orders from above, and division reports stated that we carried out strong diversionary raids. My judgment, however, was that it was not very aggressive in our sector. This was due, I believe, from the defensive complexes of the men sent on the patrols.[2]

The largest patrol started to be a secret raid of company strength in another battalion's sector. It ended up as a combat patrol of platoon strength with an FO party.[3] (I later was reprimanded for sending the FO party.) First Lieutenant Cuccinello[4] had reconnoitered the patrol route the night before with a small patrol without mishap. The patrol started out through the lines at 0100 on 28 February. The 2nd Battalion CP group went to our left OP location to observe and listen on the radios. It was a cold and tiring wait. Our first news was a call on the radio for the medic jeep to meet the patrol where they had left our lines. Another radio message came for the medics to prepare blood plasma. The patrol returned with Lieutenant Cuccinello as the casualty. He had stepped on a German Schu mine while going through the minefield near the crossroads. I do not know what the final results of his injuries were, other than the loss of part of one leg, but his injuries were not limited to just that one leg. The patrol obviously did not accomplish its mission, whatever it had been.

Other patrols helped to make our nights shorter, while we waited up for them so that we could interrogate the leaders. Only on that one patrol however, did we go up to the OP. We could almost always predict how successful a patrol would be when we saw the leader while briefing him.

One time a lot of unnecessary fuss was created by a division photo interpreter who claimed to see some self-propelled vehicles (SPs) at the edge of a wooded area to our front. We could not detect them on the same photo he used, nor could we see them from our front lines, although we could see everything in the woods. We were ordered to send out a patrol—they found no signs of any SPs ever having been there.

As I have mentioned, we were getting replacements for the losses we had suffered in January. Most of these men had been with other arms and services and had been given a short training in the ETO and sent up as riflemen. As we had the time, we gave them some last minute training before they were broken into combat duties. I instructed a class on artillery as part of the training. These classes included our organization with the infantry and a lot of emphasis on shell reports.[5] I also spent time explaining the frequent apparent premature bursts of our shells when shooting "posit" ammunition.

We established a small arms range area across the gully from the CP to zero in the rifles of our replacements and to familiarize them with other infantry weapons. It was a good idea initially but soon got out of hand when members of other units constantly requested to use it rather than establishing their own. Jeeps pulling up and personnel shooting out of the vehicles without requesting permission caused the most trouble; unanticipated gunfire caused everyone around to go into an alert mode.

REMAIN IN PLACE

As spring neared the engineers were busy patching the overloaded roads. Rubble was obtained by blasting unused buildings and ruins. Quite a bit of blasting was done in Frohmuhl on the few houses that hadn't been used for several years and were obviously not suitable for sheltering troops.

It became apparent that the Germans did not have much artillery ammunition to expend in our sector. They did use quite a bit of mortar fire, which led to us adding mortar reports to our shell reports. Then one day we did find out that they still had some heavy artillery ammunition.

As the days got longer the infantry started to feed three hot meals a day. Being that enemy activity had not bothered us in Frohmuhl, chow lines were formed despite occasional dispersion ordered by officers and non-commissioned officers. One noon, while I was talking with my men in their billets, a loud explosion interrupted us and several small objects came through the windows. At first I thought that it was the engineers blasting again, but Corporal Pine said that he heard a whine before the explosion, and we went to investigate. Sure enough, there was a shell crater in the road. The shell had missed the bridge by two yards. I assumed that the shell was of a small caliber from the crater, although later I realized the crater was small because of the hard packing of the road. The nearby chow line had dispersed.

In fifteen minutes, when the chow line had started to bunch up again, we heard another shell whine, but it was not followed by an explosion. From the accounts of various witnesses, I deduced that a shell had landed not far behind the medical aid station. As it was wet and marshy in the area, the shell had been a dud. About five minutes later there was another whine, followed by an explosion. This one was two hundred yards south of the dud and four hundred yards south of the first round.

After some time I guessed that the Germans had quit firing and went out to examine the results of the bursts of the shells that had exploded. I located the crater of the last round as well as the mark of the dud. The last round had exploded in a cultivated field and left quite a large crater. Using this information, as well as a description of the shell fragments that I had found, I telephoned in a complete shell report, which I estimated as a heavy caliber artillery shelling.

Later Captain Foster and Major Outland,[6] S-2s of the 374th FA Battalion and Division Artillery, came to follow up on my report. They wanted to dig up the dud, but we could not locate it by probing, and it would have been a messy job in that location, so the project was abandoned. From the fragments that I had collected, corps artillery personnel identified the shells as being of 210mm caliber.

That was all the shelling that we had in the several weeks we were at that location. Had the deflection been off to the left, my section and I would have been wiped out by the first round and the medics would have been casualties from the second round. Likewise, if the deflection had been to the right the bridge would have been taken out by the first round. Some shooting!

The medics were always popular with the civilians, wherever we might be. One nice warm day we were surprised to hear some young voices singing the English words to the song about sunshine. A look down the road showed us three small children, the oldest probably not over six, singing the song as they walked up the road. They had learned the song from the medics and sang it with as much feeling as if they had known what the words meant. The sound of small children's voices singing the English words to a cheerful tune had a strong emotional effect on many of us. It had been months since we had heard cheerful childish voices, it was spring, and many of us had small children at home. I had a daughter who had been born in late October, shortly after we had arrived in France.[7]

The German units in front of our sector were constantly changing. The area in front of the regiment was not conducive to good patrolling or capture of the surrendering enemy. On the other hand, the 399th Infantry to our right had regular lanes leading deserters into our lines, and we usually knew, from the trickle of deserters, which enemy units were in front of us. The sole prisoners of the 2nd Battalion were an NCO and two privates who had wandered into our lines by mistake early one morning before daylight. They were heavily loaded down with their own personal belongings—and the German soldiers really carried all sort of looted items—as well as their weapons and ammunition. From the Sixth Mountain Division, they had the mission of establishing an anti-tank position but had lost their way. The NCO acted a bit tough, and so did the men, until they were separated, then all of them loosened up a bit. Their division had been in Norway. One of their exploits was the hike across Germany to the Colmar sector. When driven out of there they had marched over to our sector.

The German bazooka, *Panzerschreck*, fascinated me.[8] It was quite a bit larger than ours, as were the rounds of ammunition. As I had fired ours, I wanted to fire one of the German variety. One spring day I got Captain Foster, a driver, and went to a safe area, where we fired it into a Maginot pillbox. It seemed to be more effective than ours but much more bulky. It was not a common weapon of the German army; however, they had plenty of the smaller single fire Panzerfausts, one of which I fired later.

The early days of spring were pleasant after the winter. We aired out all of our clothing and bedding; I had slept in my bedroll all of this time without airing it out. Generally we tried to get out into the open as much as we could on the balmy afternoons. One pastime was watching the planes overhead. Some were enemy—never more than three of these at a time—and the AAA in action added to the show, but such things were not to be watched unless one wore his steel helmet. Early in March there was increased ground activity in preparation for an Allied offensive. This, of course, brought out what planes that the Germans could find. Some damage was done by strafing planes because of our relaxed combat unit anti-aircraft defenses (fifty-caliber machine guns). One plane was flying around, and everyone left the CP to see the show; I stayed to answer any phone calls. One man ran in and asked me to identify a hot MG slug that he had picked up beside the CP. We had been strafed without most of those looking at the plane realizing the fact. Although there were bullet pockmarks all over the area, no one had been hit.

REMAIN IN PLACE

The details of the Rimling battle were just reaching us. The German division commanding officer was captured—accidentally, of course.[9] From him and other sources, it was determined that most of the 17th SS Grenadier Division had been lost in the actions around the sector. We then found that *der Fuhrer* himself had ordered the offensive.[10]

Early in March the 44th Division retook Rimling in a limited objective attack. Most of the bodies of our casualties were still there where they had fallen. Captain Maiale was called to Rimling to identify the body of one of his men—the man was known to have been killed by small arms fire, however, there was a broken-off knife in his chest. Most of the bodies were minus all or part of their clothing. The town had received much damage by our artillery since we had left it.

One day as I was leaving the CP on my way to catch up with Lieutenant Colonel Wisdom for our daily visit to the companies, a strange jeep drove up. The driver was a portly man shabbily dressed in US Army clothing. He said that he was a news correspondent and asked for permission to enter our sector.[11] We were still sensitive to the possibility of German agents in US Army uniforms since cases of such had occurred during the winter German offensives. After verifying his identity, I gave him the permission he sought.

On Sunday, February 18, I finally acted on my mother's requests and visited Private Andrew Smith[12] from my hometown. I never knew him in Iowa, but our mothers knew one another.[13] He was in a mortar squad of Mike Company, 397th Infantry.

This period of relative quiet gave us a time to meditate about the little things around us. I remember that I thought about the noises[14] and the scents[15] around me.

Notes

1. Jolly Charlie was the phonetic code for Charlie Battery of the AAA battalion.

2. Excuse my criticism of the patrolling. It was not my duty to evaluate such things, but since I mentioned it in the original manuscript, I left it there.

3. I was later reprimanded for sending the FO party on the patrol.

4. Cuccinello, Dominick, 1st Lt., Plat. Ldr., E 397 Inf. WIA.

5. Listening, counting, etc., for shell reporting data was supposed to be a way for individuals to keep their minds off of the imminent danger, about which they could not do a thing.

6. Outland, Arly L., Maj., S2, 100 Div. Arty. (formerly of 374 FA Bn.).

7. I had been informed of the birth by the American Red Cross. It was not possible during WWII for overseas military personnel to be in contact with others elsewhere by means other than mail. The American Red Cross had civilian personnel with major military organizations and throughout the United States: these could use

military communications to provide means of contact. Through these channels soldiers received timely news of births, deaths, etc.

The International Red Cross was also in the combat zone. The International Red Cross of WWII was the agency that policed the provisions of the Geneva Convention of 1929. This provided for protection of civilians in time of war, treatment of prisoners of war, and the care of the sick and wounded in the armed forces. Since Switzerland was a neutral nation during WWII, its citizens were used as members of the teams of the International Red Cross.

8. Among the papers with my manuscript was a certificate showing that I was qualified to instruct bazooka training by the 100th Division in August 1944. Sergeant Chany was the other member of the 374th Battalion so qualified.

9. After many years, I do not know what the implication was of the "of course."

10. As previously noted, we did not know much about OPERATION NORTHWIND when the original memoirs were written in 1946.

11. War correspondents, Red Cross personnel (including the doughnut girls), USO troop personnel, etc., wore army uniforms with distinctive shoulder patches. They carried identification cards showing they had rank equivalent to some army rank or grade. In case of capture they were supposed to be treated as prisoners of war and not as spies. Some uniformed civilians were provided with military jeeps, while others were accompanied by military personnel who provided transportation and other support to them.

12. Smith, Andrew, Pvt., later Cpl., M 397 Inf., from Charles City, Iowa.

13. The public relations activities of the military were very effective in keeping items in hometown newspapers relative to the activities of the military.

14. *Sounds:* wind in the pines, rattle of aluminum mess kit, digging, Burp gun fire, roar of tactical aircraft, rattle of dog tags, digging in frozen ground, plunge of a shell into a howitzer tube, crunch of footsteps in the snow, cries of the wounded, cattle mooing, rifle fire, mortar cough, total silence, field telephone ring, calls for medics, rattle of tank treads, whine of shells, aircraft, aluminum canteen chain rattle, vehicle engines, bells, sheep calling, scream of rockets, whine of truck gears, machine gun fire, drone of high flying bomber formations, pop of 20mm shell burst, whistle on a sound-power phone, objects striking a steel helmet, rifle fire, ricochets, patter of rain on a helmet liner.

15. *Smells:* cordite, pipe smoke, coal smoke, mess line gasoline heaters and suds, burning wax of C-rations, cigar smoke, freshly turned over soil, potato cellar, fermenting cabbage, gun oil, Halazone tablets, decaying human flesh, pine trees, smoke, various tobaccos, urine, perfumed letter from home, body odor, Red Cross doughnuts, cooking, vomit, burning wax, sauerkraut crocks, auto exhaust, wood smoke, bad breath, coffee, pine needles, stables, decaying animal flesh, Cosmoline, burning candles, wine, feces, cigarette smoke, medical packs, latrines.

CHAPTER 7

Pursue Northeast

By mid-March the Allies had started their offensive along the entire ETO front. Its progress had been accelerated by the capture of an intact Rhine River bridge. The Seventh Army started its move on 15 March from Lorraine in France with the 100th Division in the IV Corps. Finally, after expecting liberation from the Germans for three months, the citizens of Bitche were liberated with little resistance from the Germans. The remaining enemy forces were cleared from the area. The final move was a two day motorized move through the Hardt Mountains of Germany to the Rhine River at Ludwigshafen. On 25 March the division reverted to the XV Corps. The author accompanied the 2nd Battalion, 397th Infantry through the period.

On the morning of 15 March, the 100th Division attacked toward Bitche. The 397th Combat Team advanced east to secure Schorbach and thus cut Bitche off from the north. Easy Company moved out behind the other two battalions at 0500. As progress was favorable, the company that was on position was drawn back to Hottviller for rest and reorganization. At 1000 I heard the whine of screaming meemies. One of the rockets hit a building across the street from the CP, the explosion putting holes in communications jeeps and narrowly missing two men who had ducked into a doorway.

After I felt that that was the end of the rockets, I went on a reconnaissance to determine the caliber of the rockets—I had not learned my lesson in Guising. While examining several craters, I went into one near the road, examining the crater and searching for rocket fragments. I heard the whine of more rockets coming. Hugging the forward slope of the road embankment, I again sweated out one of those salvos. One round hit within ten yards of where I had lain, very close to the crater that I had been examining. We loaded the still hot motor housing into Private Greci's jeep and got back to the safety of the CP in a hurry. This was only a 155mm rocket, but I got just as big a scare out of the salvo as I had of the 210mm volleys in Guising.

PURSUE NORTHEAST

Later in the day I was at our OP position with Major Greene, investigating Maginot Line pill boxes in the search for a possible 374th FA Battalion CP. We had just started back to Hottviller when light German artillery started falling within fifteen yards of us. We were inside a pillbox in a hurry. The shelling walked right down the road and into town as if it were from observed fire, but the Germans no longer had observation in the sector. It was all unobserved fire obviously from well planned data.

In the afternoon I joined Lieutenant Colonel Wisdom and Captain Garden in an inspection of the Easy Company positions, northeast of Hottviller. When we passed a place where Easy Company had received its only casualties of the day, I noticed that Captain Garden was very nervous. We had to go along narrow lanes as we went through minefields that had caused the casualties in the dark. The mines had been placed in the winter and now were pushing up clods of dirt, which made the fields, especially those of the German Schu mines, easily discernable in daylight. Seeing the terrain that we had fired at for so long was of as much interest to me as seeing where Easy Company was dug in.

That evening orders came that the next morning the 2nd Battalion was to pass through the other two battalions and attack to cut the road north of Bitche and to secure the high ground north of Bitche and Camp de Bitche. It took a lot of planning, and it was late when I finally turned in, however, we were up and moving at 0315 the morning of the sixteenth. On arrival in Schorbach, another ghost town, ahead of the troops, we had to do a lot of hunting to find the 3rd Battalion CP, and then to get our troops headed in the correct direction. My instructions to my crew had been sketchy but they were chiefly concerned with getting wire to Schorbach, where I anticipated the 2nd Battalion CP would be located. I soon found myself without any of my section or a radio; I was walking along with the infantrymen.[1]

We met no opposition on the road. Around daylight we deployed in front of the most eastern company of the other battalion and advanced to the next hill, where no opposition was encountered. Since it was now daylight, we moved with more caution. When Easy Company joined us, Lieutenant William J. Law was in command; Captain William A. Garden had gone to the rear.[2]

The next obstacle was the main road that we were to cut; it was a hard surface road in a valley with open ground on both sides. Fox Company was sent to the left flank to try the least exposed route. George Company moved out to the right. As soon as Fox Company moved out, they were pinned down in an open space where every move drew German machine gun fire. George Company got across the road to an open area but drew direct fire from a tank located near where Fox Company had met trouble. Fox Company was finally able to disengage itself. We then used the chemical mortars to lay a smoke screen on the road; an inexperienced chemical corps observer had considerable trouble adjusting the fire of his smoke mortars. The remainder of the battalion crossed the open area without further trouble.

The only other opposition we encountered in reaching our objective was from

PURSUE NORTHEAST

an enemy infantryman who took one shot at George Company and then fled. The three hills that the battalion occupied were very steep, and it was quite a task to climb to the tops of them, even without opposition. Old entrenchments[3] soon were converted to foxholes for cover. Some previous occupants of the hill had carried an easy chair up there. The chair was set on a flat rock overlooking the recently captured town of Bitche, which now belonged to the 100th Division. We took turns sitting in the chair and watching the sunset over the Bitche Citadel.

My crew finally caught up with me with a wire line. Sergeant Chany and Tech 4 Bowler dug in and operated my radio near the CP. The infantry had only one telephone line to the rear CP in Schorbach, and everyone with a telephone was hooked to it. We got tired of hearing our phone ring all of the time as normal traffic went over that one line, so we used my artillery line in the CP and left the party line to the companies. The CP consisted of an old, small trench with Lieutenant Colonel Wisdom, Captain McAllister, and myself sharing it. Lieutenant Colonel Wisdom was long and lanky. Early in the evening we received a warning order, forwarded from the rear CP by Major Newton. Captain McAllister and I had a difficult time decoding the message while in prone position in a slit trench under a blanket using a flashlight. After much work and checking back on the phone, we got the general idea that we were to move to the north in the morning.

Fortunately everyone prepared cover for his entrenchment that night. I wasn't aware of any noise all night, but I discovered in the morning that I had slept through another artillery barrage. Most of the treetops around us were clipped off as a result of the artillery shelling.

The next morning, the seventeenth of March (St. Patrick's Day), the 2nd Battalion left the hills and started to assemble on the west side of the road, where we had been the morning before, in preparation to execute the orders that we were expecting. Lieutenant Colonel Wisdom went to the rear to get our orders. We were to move to Breidenbach, then to Waldhausen. Our column moved out, flushing a couple of Germans out of the woods. The most interesting part of the move to me was to see the result of harassing and interdiction artillery fires that we had delivered during the past two months. We saw several graves of recent dates, as well as seeing and smelling, at several points parts of bodies spread over considerable area.

We left the main roads because of the vehicular traffic and arrived south of Waldhausen without incident. The battalion deployed to meet any opposition we might encounter, but we found that the 397th Infantry Cannon Company was already going into position. As we were to be in reserve and as it was nearing darkness, the usual scramble for billets ensued. Our vehicles, coming by another road, started to arrive before the foot troops were entirely in town. As this was another ghost town, we had no problem with civilians. Our billets turned out to be poor, but better than a hole in the ground in a forest like the previous night.

Sunday, the eighteenth of March, found the 374th FA Battalion moving into town. Major Green was with Major Allport on reconnaissance when I saw them.[4]

63

PURSUE NORTHEAST

The 397th Regiment HQ also moved into town, and we were really starting to get crowded.

On the evening of the eighteenth, the officers and key non-commissioned officers of the 2nd Battalion had a briefing on the breaking of the Seigfried Line. An officer from the 100th Division staff had gone further north along the US front where the Seigfried Line had been broken and had observed the details of the construction of the fortifications and talked to several units that had used various methods to pass through it. At that time the line to our front had not been broached, and it looked like we might be the spearhead if the 100th Division had to fight through it. Just incidentally, the briefing was given to a group bunched on the top of a hill above the town—a nice target if the enemy could see and had artillery to shell the group. The Germans did shell that area a couple of nights later.

On the afternoon of 19 March, the 397th Infantry was relieved and the 2nd Battalion moved to the village of Schweyen. I took a couple of my section in one of our jeeps and went back to visit the town of Bitche. On our way back we passed some screaming meemie ammunition dumps, and we stopped to get a close look at the rockets. We moved on to the 155mm rocket launcher position from which Hottviller had been shelled a few days previously. This was my first chance to examine one of the launchers close up and to see a typical firing position.

We then went into the town of Bitche, circling the hill that contained the Citadel, and then drove up the lone narrow road into the top.[5] Bitche Citadel had been carved out of a sandstone mountain, including its ramparts and the usual outer parts that can be seen from the distance. The interior of the fortification was caves carved out of rock; it was in these that the civilians of the town lived for the three months that they waited liberation. On the flat top area were a few structures that could not be in the caves: ammunition storage, bakery, etc. The top area was only used as an AAA position and for observation by the Germans, but we had shelled it as if it were the bastion of the enemy army. The Wehrmacht had escaped the shelling by operating from Camp de Bitche (Hindenburg Kaserne, to the occupying Germans). The fortification was in fairly good shape, despite its age and the fact we had shelled it for about four months. The top was a very good location for observation posts to see the area around the town.

On the afternoon of the 20 March the regiment was relieved and the 2nd Battalion moved to the village of Schweyen. Like Waldhausen, it was just on the French side of the border; we were not yet in Germany. That night Waldhausen, and especially Baker Battery, 374th FA Battalion, received a heavy shelling by light German artillery, which we took as an indication that the enemy was using up his ammunition prior to his withdrawing. The 3rd Division on our left had attacked the Seigfried Line and had gone through it with little effort.

On the twenty-first I visited the CP of the 3rd Division Artillery, located near us in Schweyen. The news was that the Third Army was rapidly driving from the north across the Sarr-Palatinate, toward us, and I asked if they were in artillery range of us yet. They were not, but the possibility of it happening had been considered.[6]

PURSUE NORTHEAST

There was not much activity for us that day, but things sure picked up for me that night! Some time during the night we received a warning order that we were to move out in the morning. I took a cold ride in the early morning hours, picking up maps from the 374th FA Battalion CP, getting copies of 2nd Battalion orders from the regimental HQ, alerting the kitchens, etc. This was not the duty of an artillery liaison officer. As soon as we had digested the orders at the 2nd Battalion, we had a company officers meeting to issue the battalion order.

We were to be the advance guard of the regiment, with the Rhine as the objective. Our attachments were enough to make us a balanced combat task force: tanks, tank destroyers, Able Battery of the 374th FA Battalion, engineers, etc. With the infantry on trucks, tanks, TDs, etc., we were to be fully motorized.

Sunrise the morning of the twenty-second found us, a bit sleepy, trying to assemble all of the vehicles and men at the jump-off point. Reconnaissance, made before the task force move, found the Seigfried Line unoccupied but crater blown in the road and located to prevent vehicular movement. The engineers had to fill the craters before we could move out. Finally, at noon, we moved out.

The move was full of stops and starts as we frequently ran into blown bridges, craters, etc. Our liaison section trailer, improvised during our stay in Frohmuhl, was in danger of tipping over every time that it hit a rough spot in the road. Sergeant Chany and Tech 5 O'Rourke were frequently out of the wire jeep, running along side the trailer to steady it. I think that they came as near as anyone in the US Army to winning the dubious distinction of covering the most territory in the Rhineland-Pfalz (Palatinate) on foot.

As soon as we crossed into Germany there was much interest in the civilians, condition of roads and buildings, etc. This was the enemy, and here was his home. Many men, here and elsewhere we went in the country, had small moustaches, Hitler style. The Seigfried Line had been abandoned in our sector. Only isolated German soldiers were to be found, usually coming out of the woods to surrender after the head of the column had passed them. We skirted the edge of Pirmasens, turning directly north. We reached an overpass above a railroad track and creek which, we found, was not strong enough to carry our tanks. We tried to bypass it, but after two tanks got through the third one dropped into it. Much effort was spent in trying to get the tank out and to prepare another bypass, but to no avail. After dark the effort was given up; we left the tank and doubled back to Pirmasens, where we bedded down in a former Wehrmacht barracks. It was 2330 when we laid down our bedrolls on the cement floors. Our first night in Germany was not very comfortable.[7]

On the morning of the twenty-third we pulled out of our bivouac at 0800, left Pirmasens by another road, and met the elements of our task force that had gotten past the overpass the previous night. We soon encountered the ruins of Wehrmacht columns that the Air Corps had caught on the road and strafed. There were not many motor vehicles; most of the columns had been horse drawn. There were still a few loose horses running around, but most of them had been killed. A lot of the motor vehicles had not been hit but simply had run out of gas and been abandoned. An American jeep, painted Wehrmacht gray, had been hit and burned; two Germans in it had been well taken care of by the hot fire which must have been fed by gasoline.

We found three civilian-type radios, which we loaded into our already crowded jeep with the intention of fixing at least one to be the section radio. This project never worked out, however. Corporal Pine wanted to tow a nice-looking civilian car stalled along the side of the road, but I would not let him, although many of the other vehicles in our column had such spoils in tow.

The task force made a prolonged stop by a lumber mill and tavern while waiting for clearance to take a certain road. The buildings had been used by the Germans for a corps, or higher echelon, headquarters. We found all sorts of communications equipment, such as teletypes, etc.[8] I even managed to get a German colonel's uniform, which I eventually sent back to the States.

During this advance we constantly had at least one artillery liaison plane overhead of our task force at all times during daylight hours. These served several needs. They acted as eyes for column, notifying us of obstacles coming up, they served as radio relay stations, and they kept the higher headquarters informed as to the status of the column.[9]

We moved through Neustadt, where I saw for the first time some of the US Army tanks equipped with multiple rocket launchers—they had arrived by a different route than we had used. On leaving Neustadt we came out of the wooded mountains and into the low-level Rhine River Valley, very pleasant to behold, with its fields just starting to grow.[10] We finally located the 2nd Battalion CP in Assenheim, and the task force was disbanded. I went in search of the 374th FA Battalion, knowing that they had moved behind the task force. I did find Captain Lind, who was on a reconnaissance for a CP location.

That night, for the first time in a long time, we slept in comfortable beds. It was the first time we were able to order civilians out of their houses, and we started to enjoy the privileges of being conquerors. Except for a few isolated spots, the Sarrland and Palatinate were in Allied hands, the last area west of the Rhine to be cleared of German troops.

The companies, using jeep patrols, maintained patrols during the night. In the morning one of How Company's jeeps hit a mine on a road that they had been using all night. On the morning of the twenty-fourth, the 2nd Battalion was ordered to move to Schifferstadt. The move was by foot. I started to follow riding in my jeep but was soon afoot, marching with the troops. It was a warm day, and field jackets were soon shed. We took over a section of the town as our billet area, much to the dismay of the inhabitants. We soon found out that they thought that we were ordering them out so that we could burn that section of town.[11] All of the houses were well kept, with good furnishings, etc. Part of the reason was the fact that each household had at least one person, of Polish or other displaced nationality, as

PURSUE NORTHEAST

"hired help." These people might claim that they were not Nazis, but they surely hadn't suffered when the Nazis were running their country.[12]

No sooner than we had gotten nicely settled in our new location than orders arrived, telling us to turn our sector over to the 1st Battalion 398th Infantry. That was the organization that I had been with in Guising in January. The advance party arrived almost as soon as our orders, and I spent a few minutes with them discussing happenings since I had last seen them. By 1600 they had taken over, and we started to move to Oggersheim, arriving after dark. I found that the 374th FA Battalion CP was only one block from the 2nd Battalion CP.

As there were no German army units between the Rhine and us, a rather effective barrier, we were the nearest to being out of the line as we had been. For 146 consecutive days the division had been on line. March twenty-fifth was Palm Sunday and seemed appropriately quiet. For a few days the 1st and 3rd Battalions were in Ludwigshafen and had to avoid machine gun and mortar fire from across the Rhine. The 2nd Battalion was engaged in ridding itself of winter equipment and taking hikes; the short marches we had taken the twenty-fourth had shown the troops to be in poor physical condition. I took some jeep rides around the area, including one into Ludwigshafen, which had been well worked over by the air corps. I started to gain respect for the Strategic Air Command, but I still cannot understand why there were so many duds in the area. The IG Farber plant, except for the office building, had been well worked over. The factory office, so we were told, had been spared on order, and SHEAF officers had taken over most of this, making it off limits. The records were presumably being searched.[13]

In my travels I saw a column of American half-tracks that had been caught by anti-tank fire. They were in line, evenly spaced, along a dike besides the river. Each had one large anti-tank hole in the river side of the tank facing the river. That would have made an interesting photograph.[14]

Because of the size and military importance of both Ludwigshafen and Mannheim, just across the Rhine, the area had extensive AAA defenses, only surpassed in my later travel by those of Munich. The installations were located for miles around the urban area.

After a few days with the 2nd Battalion, I returned with my section and the FO parties to the 374th FA Battalion. We got rid of excesses and winter equipment, reorganized, and traded our makeshift trailer for a regulation issue one. The three liaison officers prepared a SOP for our FOs, incorporating Major Allport's ideas.

Everyone caught up on their mail.[15]

I was given a seven-day pass and arrived in Brussels on Easter morning, April 1, 1945.

PURSUE NORTHEAST

Notes

1. While in the vicinity, I was told that I should have a look at something different. It was an impressive structure filled with human bones. As there had been recent pictures in the newspapers of piles of human bones found in German concentration camps, the first impression of all was that this might also be a site of atrocities, but the medical personnel consulted estimated that the bones were up to three centuries old; that eliminated that possibility. The structure was an ossuary. Later we found out that ossuary's were not uncommon in France, for a variety of reasons.

2. My original manuscript did not say why Captain Garden had gone back, but this was unusual.

3. The old entrenchments probably were made by the Germans in 1940, when they were stopped by the Maginot Line fortifications, before France capitulated. We had found similar entrenchments south of Bitche in December.

4. I had encountered Major Allport before. In July 1943, I was the CO of HQ Battery, 375th FA Battalion for three weeks, and Major Allport had been assigned to the 375th and made their S-3 during that period.

5. The town and Citadel of Bitche were considered to have been liberated when 100th Division troops entered the town streets on the 16th of April. The departing Germans fired only five rifle shots at the officer and six men who entered town.

The liberators were welcomed by the residents of Bitche with much enthusiasm. The people came out into the warmth and sunshine of spring after a harsh winter in caves. These people were found to be in dire striates. The Civil Affairs agencies rushed food and other necessities into the town as soon as possible. Medical help was provided.

The Liberation was later celebrated in ceremonious fashion with the 100th Division Commanding General being designated as an honorary citizen of Bitche.

The association of the 100th Division with the Bitche region, and the related slang term for a dog, led to the formation of "The Society of the Sons of Bitche" as an informal designation for the Division Association.

6. Where there are situations where fire might fall on friendly forces in our sector, we put no-fire lines on our overlays to remind us not to shoot in that direction.

7. We had gotten used to being conquerors, with the power to evict the civilians and to use their houses for quarters. We used the army barracks, as we would have in friendly locations.

8. At the tactical level we did not look for communications equipment that could be of high strategical value. Having teletype equipment indicated that the site was not of immediate tactical concern, so we were not interested in it. That location might have had code machines, but we had not been asked to look for such items and thus did not concern ourselves with them.

9. This assistance to friendly ground movement was only possible when the slow, unarmed planes were free of possible enemy fire from the ground or air. Thus, it was only available for this pursuit through the Hardt Mountains of all the time we were in combat.

PURSUE NORTHEAST

10. When we broke out into the Rhine Valley, Corporal Pine remarked that it looked like the Mississippi River Valley. I remembered that he had come from Southern Illinois, where he had seen the Mississippi often. Not many of our personnel came from regions far from the east coast.

11. They may have been expecting the worst because of German propaganda telling them that the Allies would do this if they were able to defeat the Wehrmacht, or it may have been expected because they knew that German troops had done such when they entered another country.

12. The contrast between the rural, looted, and long-occupied France and the urban, long-victorious Germany was great.

13. We did not have any idea as to what intelligence was being sought. Some of it, we found out much later, was the search for any information of the extent of German nuclear research.

14. During WWII photographs were mostly black and white. Color photography was available, but was not in wide use. Official photographers were members of the Signal Corps who had field developing and printing facilities. Self-developing cameras were not yet invented. Censorship regulations were strict and news correspondents had their developed film and prints censored. Personal cameras, like private diaries, were forbidden, but individuals managed to acquire cameras, find film, and develop and print photographs.

15. Since the country started the US Mail service in the nineteenth century, the military has delivered mail to and from the service men. The civilian postal system delivered the mail to the military system, which then delivered the mail to the individual. Mail home went the reverse route.

The delivery of mail to the military was made by a mail clerk. Each company (infantry), troop (cavalry), or battery (artillery) unit had such a clerk who was designated to receive, sort, and distribute the unit mail. When the distribution was to be made, the words "mail call" rang out. The term goes back to the early horse-transported army where sounding the bugle call of "mail call" made the announcement.

V-mail was created during WWII to expedite the movement of mail across long distances. Special one page forms were used and furnished through supply channels to the service personnel overseas. After completion and censoring, the forms were sealed and put into the military mail system. (Military personnel overseas did not have to use stamps. Their signature sufficed to transmit their mail.) At postal centers the V-mail form was opened and photographed on microfilm. After air transmittal to he United States, the microfilm was developed, enlarged, and resulting letter sent to its destination by the Post Office. Saving in space permitted air transmittal from the combat zone to the states by air and gave better delivery times than that of surface mail. The final delivered small reproduction was not something that gave a very personal feeling.

CHAPTER 8

Capture Heilbronn

On the first of April the Allied Forces continued their offensive along the entire ETO front and were able to cross the Rhine River at several points. The 100th Division was assigned the mission of crossing the Neckar River and capturing the city of Heilbronn. This was an industrial city in between the river and German heights that offered observation for massive artillery fires. The enemy forces wee an array of last-ditch manpower. The city was reduced to a pile of rubble by the intense artillery fires and aerial bombing that resulted from the battle. The author accompanied the 2nd Battalion, 397th Infantry as it captured its sector of the city.

Early in April 1945, the newspapers were full of speculation about an Alpine redoubt and a German last stand. Items speculated about trained "werewolves" left through Germany to sabotage the conquering armies. The allies had agreed on their terms for a peace pact and the division of conquered Germany into sectors. Allied forces were moving to meet at prior agreed lines.

The 100th Division was able to cross the Rhine, swollen by spring rains and melting snows, on 31 March from Ludwigshafen to Mannheim. The crossing was via a pontoon bridge.

April first, Easter Sunday, the division moved out, passing over the Rhine River valley plain and into the Neckar Valley. The mission was to pursue the German forces to the southeast, shuffling with other divisions for sectors and to protect flanks. Strong points were encountered and reduced. A few cultural centers, such as the university city of Heidelberg, were not defended and thus spared from aerial bombardment and shelling. The passive defense measures of mines, blown bridges, and roadblocks slowed movement throughout the region. Road mines took out many 100th Division vehicles. There was so much confusion in the area of advance that Division Artillery Headquarters gave very strict orders against artillery fires.

CAPTURE HEILBRONN

For the 397th Infantry, casualties were very light. They captured many prisoners: 337 on the first, 1080 on the second, and 274 on the third. This gave a total of 1691 for the three days.

This period ended on the afternoon of 3 April. On the fourth the situation changed from pursuit to attack for the 397th Combat Team. The 2nd Battalion began to cross the Neckar River in the afternoon of the fourth and drew concentrated artillery fire. The apparently quiet city of Heilbronn erupted into a strongpoint. The combined disadvantages of a river crossing and street fighting called for the support masses of artillery and aerial bombardment to support the infantry movements. On mid-day of the fifth, the 3rd Battalion of the 397th Infantry crossed into another sector of Heilbronn. The 1st Battalion entered at a third sector of the city on the evening of the fifth.

During the next few days, infantry progress was behind artillery supporting fires. Smoke generators were used to provide screens concealing the engineer efforts to get crossings for armored vehicles. By the tenth tanks and tank destroyers had been ferried across the Neckar.

I rejoined the 374th again on 7 April on my return from pass to Brussels. After quite a bit of searching, I found and rejoined the 374th FA Battalion in Frankenback. I learned that a wire jeep from HQ Battery had hit a mine at Sinsheim on 4 April, killing Lieutenant Slayline and Private First Class Von Hegel.[1] The jeep driver, Private First Class Matts, had been injured and was returned to the States because of his injuries. This was the second time that he had been driving a jeep that had hit a road mine.[2] A Charlie Battery jeep had also struck a mine, slightly injuring three.

On Sunday, the eighth of April, I rejoined the rear CP of the 2nd Battalion in Neckargartach and relieved Captain Alton G. Williams,[3] who had been acting as LnO-2 in my place. The 242nd Field Artillery Battalion, a light artillery battalion, was attached to the 374th FA Battalion and had one of its FOs in my sector.

Some changes had occurred in the 2nd Battalion. Lieutenant Henderson was no longer with the battalion. Captain Maiale was now the regimental S-3, and First Lieutenant Vincent A. Laudone[4] now commanded How Company. Captain Stallworth had been wounded, and Lieutenant Bradshaw had taken over as commander of Fox Company, only to be killed the same day. On an operational basis, Captain McAllister now operated in the rear CP rather than up at the forward CP as he had while we were west of the Rhine.

The situation on the eighth found the 100th Division on the west bank of the Neckar River in the vicinity of Heilbronn. All the Neckar bridges were blown. The plan had been for the 397th Infantry to cross the river and clear the city, the 398th Infantry to cross south of the city, and the 399th Infantry to revert to the reserve. Our medics had received unusually heavy casualties, and it was surmised that the city defenders were not observing the Geneva Conference rules concerning firing at medics wearing red crosses.[5]

The enemy held high ground behind the city of Heilbronn. They could look for

CAPTURE HEILBRONN

miles to our rear and had plenty of artillery and rockets to back up this observation with accurate fire. Artillery fire was drawn on both front and rear areas. We had a river to cross. The only means of crossing the river was by ferry, despite repeated attempts by the engineers to build a bridge. Ferrying sites were subject to disrupting artillery fire. Tanks with rubber floats were brought up but never made a crossing after two of them capsized and sank while attempting to get into the water. Extensive use of smoke screens was made to minimize the German observation.

On the morning of Sunday the eighth, while I was getting familiar with the situation, an officer came into the CP and wanted to know where the 2nd Battalion wanted his fires for the day placed. I learned that he commanded a platoon of rocket launching tanks. After being shot once, it took a day to clean his material and to prepare it for another salvo. We decided that he had one of the easiest jobs at the front.[6]

On the afternoon of the eighth, Lieutenant Colonel Wisdom decided to move to the forward CP across the river. The location was in a house used as a forward switching central by the battalion wire section. My place was at the forward CP with him. We decided that we would take his jeep and one of mine with us. I took Corporal Pine and Private First Class Cooper with me; Tech 4 Bowler, my regular radio operator, was on pass. We moved vehicles and personnel to the ferry site, and the engineers got the ferry ready. The two jeeps were driven onto the ferry and then the personnel boarded. When we were half-way across, we knew that we had been seen as German artillery shells started to hit and burst in the water around us. We wasted no time in unloading when we got to the far bank. I got into my jeep, and we kept going after we were off the ferry, although the infantry group kept under cover until the fire lifted. Not knowing where we were going, we finally found the 1st Battalion CP and were directed to the location of the 2nd Battalion forward CP party; we had to retrace our steps a bit. Nothing of importance happened until that night, when we received a heavy shelling. We sent the forward CP personnel to the basement, where they were able to sleep until morning. The Colonel and I stayed upstairs. The night was red due to the fires around us.

The next day, the ninth, offered a chance for us to look around the area. We did not have to look far to find dead, either friendly or enemy. The graves registration detail came across the river that day but found that they had too much to do without the help of their vehicles and with all of the exposure to enemy fire. My men had laid a telephone wire across the river before I arrived, but it had not yet been put to use. We extended that wire to the forward CP and installed our section's switchboard.

As none of the troops had received any hot food since crossing the river, plans were made to get hot chow across the river that night. As the 2nd Battalion had only the battalion commander's jeep across the river, I offered my jeep to assist in hauling the chow from the ferry landing to the CP, with Corporal Pine as the driver. While the chow was being unloaded from the ferry, the Germans threw a salvo of rockets at the ferry site. Corporal Pine rushed away from the landing in the jeep

72

CAPTURE HEILBRONN

and, in making a turn in the road, he drove off of the road, turning the jeep over and hurting his back. He did not have any of the chow on his jeep as the 2nd Battalion Weasel had been on the ferry carrying the rations and supplies.[7] The food was cold when it got to the men, but it was good after having been on C-rations for a while

The morning of the tenth, we found that we could move in daylight without the Germans throwing artillery fire at us, so we used the Weasel to right the overturned jeep and to tow it back to the ferry. Corporal Pine went back across the river to have his back taken care of, and Private Collins came up to take his place. During the day I fulfilled my desire and fired a Panzerfaust. Toward the end of the day the 2nd and 3rd Battalions established contact and consolidated their two bridgeheads, which were more like toeholds, into one.

During the night of 10 April, Lieutenant Colonel Wisdom and I returned to the rear CP where we caught up on our sleep. During that night the engineers put some tanks and TDs across the river. We returned to the east side of the river in the morning; I took Tech 5 O'Rourke and Private Southard with me.

We went up to see the start of the attack of the day to the company making it. My wire crew, O'Rourke and Southard, laid wire by hand behind us. We had to do some fancy running across open streets and past open spaces to avoid the small arms fire that we drew. Add street fighting to the training for artillery liaison personnel![8]

After some delays we got our share of the tanks that had crossed during the night, and the attack was ready to start. I had the 242nd FA Battalion's forward observer adjust and fire a preparation for the attack. He fired his own battalion and, after some tough luck in the adjustment, he fired the preparation and left with the attacking company.[9]

It was not long before we heard the noises of a firefight, and we were happy to hear the fire of our tanks in the fight. A battalion headquarters company wireman was reported as killed before the first strong point had been reduced. It was not long until we started to get captured Germans being sent back to us at the CP. By night the 100th Division had cleaned out the better part of our sector of the city.[10]

On the twelfth we received word that President Roosevelt had died. Captain Foster came up to visit me at the forward CP, and I learned that Major Allport was spending most of his time at the 2nd Battalion rear CP. Sergeant Chany and Private First Class Cooper came up to join me. Tech 5 O'Rourke and Private Southard went to the rear. The city was reported as being completely cleared that morning. It was nearly leveled, with only the church spire and a similar spire of a nearby building left standing.

In the afternoon we were ordered to send a patrol to the hill and tower overlooking the city.[11] Colonel Wisdom established his OP in a textile warehouse where we could see the tower, and I extended my telephone lines to the OP. As Fox Company patrol was about to jump-off, word came to hold it, as the Division Artillery Commanding General had ordered an artillery TOT on the top of the hill before it was taken. The TOT was fired, and the patrol went up the hill to the castle.

CAPTURE HEILBRONN

No opposition was met, and twelve prisoners were taken—these were found asleep in trenches at the top of the hill. The TOT or the air bombardment that the tower had received previously had done little damage.[12]

While at the OP we could see tactical aircraft working over a ground target in the distance. We ended the day by sending the rest of Fox Company and the tanks to the top of the hill. The 397th Anti-Tank Company figured in the day.[13] That night we received orders to take the rest of the 2nd Battalion to the same high ground in the morning.

Heilbronn was ours. From intelligence reports, we learned that a German Lieutenant General who had given orders to his troops to hold or die conducted the defense. We had leveled nearly every building in the city, and it was reported that for months the stench of death hung over the ruins.[14]

Notes

1. All four of the KIA personnel from Headquarters Battery, 374th FA Battalion are buried in the Lorraine American Cemetery at St. Avold, Moselle, France. Private First Class Von Hegel's grave is adjacent to that of Lieutenant Slayline.

2. I found out, much later, that Private First Class Matts returned home crippled.

3. Williams, Alton G., Capt., Asst. S-3, 374th FA.

4. Laudone, Vincent A., 1st Lt., H-397.

5. Generally the German soldiers had previously observed the Geneva Conventions in respect to not firing on medical personnel. We were now opposed by a fanatic collection of Volkssturm, Hitler Youth, stragglers, and other irregulars who may have had no such reservations. Also, it may be that civilians were shooting at our medics during the fighting in Heilbronn.

6. It has been noted in earlier chapters that German rocket launchers took only a few minutes to reload and fire another salvo. The rockets used by the armies in WWII were limited to tactical applications where blast or penetration was needed. All rockets had impact exploded fuses. Blast rockets were high explosive missiles. Penetrating missiles used shaped charges and were usually used for anti-tank applications.

The rockets were stabilized in flight by fins (anti-tank missiles) or by the spin imparted by angled exhaust gas orifices in the tail of the rockets. Rockets were launched from either single tube launchers (single use, discarded or reusable) or multi-tube launchers. Multi-tube launchers could be mounted on trailers, tanks, landing craft, etc. Before the war ended, rocket field artillery battalions had been formed; they had trailer-mounted twenty-four-tube launchers.

7. The M-29 Weasel was new to us. It was a two-ton tracked amphibious cargo carrier, with wide rubber tracks.

8. Field artillery liaison and forward observer personnel may have been with the

CAPTURE HEILBRONN

infantry personnel in field exercises, but I do not know of them being trained with the infantry when the infantry took training in such things as street fighting.

9. I am sure that the poor performance of the 242nd FA Battalion FO reflected on the 374th's reputation in the eyes of the supported infantry.

10. Three units from the 100th Division were awarded Distinguished Unit Citations for their participation in capturing Heilbronn: 1st Battalion, 397th Infantry Regiment; 2nd Battalion, 398th Infantry Regiment; and 3rd Battalion, 397th Infantry Regiment.

11. I can remember that the side of the hill to be climbed looked very un-war-like. It was covered with patches of gardens and occasional wooden tool sheds, with green crops just starting to sprout.

12. This same tower had been the scene of an action by the 398th Infantry a few days earlier.

13. During the Heilbronn battle, the 397th AT Company was used as a rifle company. There was little need for their AT guns.

14. Another view of the Heilbronn battle may be found in Bowman, B. Lowery and Mosher, Paul F., *op. cit.*

CHAPTER 9

Attack South

The Allied forces in the ETO were continuing their offensive into the heart of Germany. To the north they were rapidly advancing to meet the Russians, and to the south to meet the Allied forces. The Century Division was assigned to take Stuttgart by sweeping the area between the Neckar River and the Lowenstein Hills; the 397th Combat Team was assigned that center of that sector. The author again accompanied the 2nd Battalion, 397th Infantry as it was temporarily cut off from the rest of the rest of the regiment, then as it swept their sector into Stuttgart area. On 26 April, the 100th Division left the VI Corps for Seventh Army Reserve, ending its days in combat and starting its duties as an Occupation Force.

Early one morning on Friday the thirteenth of April (the only Friday the thirteenth that the 100th Division had during combat) the rifle companies of the 2nd Battalion moved up onto the hill northeast of Heilbronn. Plans were made to move the forward CP up with the rest of the battalion, and the laying of telephone wires up the hill was started; however, orders came for the battalion to move on the road to Weinsberg and then south. A pontoon bridge had been put over the Neckar River in Heilbronn, and vehicles started to appear on our side. The rest of our section joined me, as did the FO vehicles.

It took quite a bit of coordination to get the rifle companies and the tanks down from the hills in proper order and then to get the battalion vehicles and the attached TDs into their places in the column. I left my wire jeep to extend my wire, until it became apparent that wire laying was useless. It also soon became apparent, after several road mines had to be removed along our route but no active opposition was obvious, that we were in an approach march situation.

I walked with the column except when we went into town, and then I rode my jeep again. In Weinsberg all of the buildings flew white flags and all of the villagers were out along the street to see their conquerors.[1] My jeep was the center of

ATTACK SOUTH

attention—it was the first jeep in the column, up with the tanks and TDs, and presumably the first jeep that they had seen.[2] Weinsberg was still burning from the TAC bombing of the day before, and many were crying about their losses.[3] We had to detour around the center of town because of the bombing damage.

We had some light rain that day, but the weather had been favorable for air observation since the 100th Division had crossed the Rhine. Liaison planes were overhead giving us good help by radio as to detours around roadblocks, blown bridges, etc.

We encountered some snipers on the edge of the woods between Lehrensteinsfeld and Obr Heinriet; these were taken under direct fire from our tanks. After the snipers had been dispersed, the troops proceeded in the woods along the roads. The tracked vehicles bypassed a crater in the road, but we had to send the wheeled vehicles back to Lehrensteinsfeld to wait, as we expected the crater to be repaired soon. I did not even dismount my radio and walked along with the riflemen. Progress through the wood was without incident until we heard some screaming meemies launching. We took cover, but the rockets were intended for some unit to our right. Our change of direction to the south after Heilbronn apparently had confused the Germans.

We met some opposition in taking Obr Heinriet. While they had not been organized for a defense of the town, the fire of several Panzerfaust rounds gave us both killed and wounded casualties. In return we captured a total of 92 POWs. It was dark before the entire battalion was in town and defenses were set up for the night. Word was received that the crater in the woods had an unexploded bomb in it, and the engineers would have to work on it before our tracked vehicles could get to us. That meant that it would be at least morning before we could get food and evacuate some of the causalities who needed attention. I was without a radio, and the FOs were having difficulty contacting our battalion with their radios.

The electric current was still on in the village. Our troops were taking advantage of that rare event[4] and enjoying it. Despite warnings the blackout precautions were very poor. When it became apparent to the German forces that we had lights, a high velocity gun, or tank perhaps, fired several rounds into the town, and electrical power was lost.

The morning of the fourteenth found us in Obr Heinriet, with no supply/evacuation route to the rear. Some wounded men were dying because of the lack of adequate medical attention. We had left Heilbronn after a hard battle and without rest or having been resupplied. The ammunition supply was low. The tanks and TDs needed both fuel and ammunition. We radioed our situation to the rear CP, still in Neckargartach, stating that we were unable to move until we could get supplies and evacuate both our wounded and our prisoners.

By radio the news from the rear was that the engineers were prevented from working on the road crater by small arms fire. The enemy had gotten into the woods, and they were between us and the rest of the US Army. A suggested solution from

ATTACK SOUTH

the rear CP was for us to send our tanks and some infantry back to pick up supplies at the crater—that showed that the rear CP (now in Lehrensteinsfeld) really did not know our situation, and they were told that it was not possible.

That morning the town was divided into sectors for defense, ammunition was redistributed, and troops were moved to defensive position around the town. We soon found that his had been a wise move as the Germans were not content only to have us cut off; they wanted to overcome us. At 1550 we were hit from all directions in a coordinated attack. The attack was supported by artillery and rocket fire, causing considerable damage to the town. The FOs used radio via a liaison plane relay to bring friendly artillery fire into the area. Artillery fire, plus the direct fire of the tanks and TDs, permitted our defenders to reverse the initiative and to capture more prisoners, but our meager supply of ammunition was nearly depleted.

We received word that the 1st Battalion was attempting to break through to us by clearing the vicinity of the crater and following our route of the previous evening. We soon heard the sounds of their fight, but it looked like they would not reach us before dark. At 1900 we were asked by radio if we wished supplies to be dropped by plane. It was almost dark, and they would only be able to drop enough for us to hold out but not enough for us to move on. By 1750 our "Affirmative" reply to the question was give a "Roger," but by then it was too dark to act on it. We prepared to spend another night where we were, but with very gloomy prospects.

At 2150 we were startled when the 1st Battalion CO and his staff arrived at the CP. The 1st Battalion was coming into town, and the road crater had been repaired. Using the two jeeps that had arrived with the 2nd Battalion, the wounded who had not died were immediately sent to the rear. Soon 2nd Battalion vehicles were arriving with our much-needed supplies. Wire was soon laid to us. Collins and Cooper arrived with my radio jeep. We managed to sleep easier that night than we had the previous night.

On the morning of Sunday, the fifteenth of April, we were ordered to move to Unt Heinriet. As the first elements were about to move out, Major Allport called me and offered all the artillery support that we might need. We called for a preparation that delayed the attack some. The attack did start at 1000. This time I took my radio jeep with the assault troops when they left town. Soon the Germans became aware of our intent, and we had to take cover from their artillery fires. Two concentrations in my sector of the assault did no damage. At 1145 the town of Unt Heinriet was ours after offering light resistance.

The rear CP personnel joined us, and the 2nd Battalion started to set up the first complete CP that we had in some time. My section was complete and with me again. The TDs got their much-needed supplies. The battalion had not received a break since they had entered Heilbronn, and they started to settle into the battered town—it had been hit by TAC a few days earlier.[5] We had expectations of being given a rest, but orders came for us to move. I had one of my jeeps go to the rear of the column and sought out the march CP on foot. We left town toward wood to the east. A light caliber SP gun was interdicting the town from these woods. I had one

ATTACK SOUTH

of the FOs adjust artillery fire on the SP gun and harass it by shelling until the battalion was in the woods. We did not wait for this fire to neutralize the SP gun, and the column moved across open ground in front of it. No casualties were received since we used all possible defilade to shield us.

The road we followed in the woods had been a lumber trail and had not received much recent use. It took close study of the map to keep us located because of the many side trails. We had a scary trip through those woods—it would have been a good place for an ambush. Soon we could hear artillery firing from all positions in all directions around us, and we knew that it was not our artillery. We were moving among German gun positions. The head of the column sighted two enemy command vehicles and knocked them out with tank fire, but their occupants escaped.

One company left the column to see if the village of Vorhof was clear; they drew artillery fire. I was asked to check to see if the artillery were friendly. I went to the rear of the column to use the radio on my jeep, but the jeep was not there. Neither was the FO party that had been firing to protect our movement. Using the radio of another FO party in the column, I found out that it was not our artillery that was firing at Vorhof, and thus it was the Germans firing. While on the radio I gave our position to the FDC and then had to check on it, as they did not believe it to be correct. We had surprised both friend and enemy in moving the direction we did.

We moved into Etzlensmenden, where we again encountered enemy artillery fire. Our arrival there was a surprise to the Germans, and we captured six officers and twenty-six men; some of these were from an artillery CP and the rest were replacements on their way to the front. Some of them were captured when they unsuspectingly came into town on bicycles after we were there.[6] We closed the entire battalion into the town as it was getting dark, around 2000 hours.

We were again running out of supplies, however, we told the rear CP to wait until morning to send supplies through the woods. This was the first time that Lieutenant Colonel Wisdom ate non-issue food—he joined us in eating foraged foods.

On the morning of 16 April we were waiting further orders. I was commenting in the CP about not having a Lugar pistol for a souvenir. Shortly after that I was at an OP on the hill above the town when I saw a German officer walking toward our lines with his hands above his head. I ran to meet him, but it was in vain; he had walked into our lines before I reached him, and one of the riflemen had his Lugar. Going back to the CP I was told that one of the HQ Company men had found a Lugar in the building, only about a yard from where I had slept the previous night.[7]

At 1130 we received orders to go slowly until other units caught up with us. Of course we agreed with the sensibility of such an order, but every time we had gotten ahead of the others it had been the result of orders. We learned that the unit on our right was meeting stiff opposition. We set out to clean out the small towns bordering the cultivated valley to our front.

Easy Company moved out towards Kaiserbach, and we soon learned that the

ATTACK SOUTH

enemy had observation of the open valley and any movement drew artillery fire. As soon as Kaiserbach had been taken Fox Company moved Billingsbach, skirting the exposure in the valley, and took this objective by midnight.

In the meantime attempts to supply us had been made. Wheeled vehicles were not able to cover the forest trail. Attempts were made using Weasels. After two Weasels broke down, a third was able to make it with a huge load of varied supplies and equipment. Private First Classes Collins and Cooper came on the Weasel with an SCR-609 radio set for me. The infantry was supplied with an artillery SCR-694 radio set.[8] That was carried with the forward elements thereafter and provided much better communications with the rear.

I learned from my men that the reason my section had not been in the rear of the column was that they had missed it. (All the other vehicles had also missed it.) The FO had not followed orders to join the column and had stayed in Unt Heinriet after covering us with his fires. In the meantime I had arranged for the Cannon Company FO party to be with the rifle company that was short an FO.

On 17 April another road to Etzlensmenden was cleared, and our rear elements joined us. The regimental AT Company also came up to operate as a rifle company with us.[9] As soon as the remainder of my section arrived, I moved out on foot, with a small party, to join Lieutenant Colonel Wisdom in Billingsbach. The party consisted of the Cannon Company liaison officer and his party, Lieutenant Laudone and his party, and myself with Private First Classes Collins and Cooper. We got too far down into the valley and received several volleys of light artillery fire, which did little more then make us shaky. After that fire ceased, we moved on what we thought was the right route, only to be pinned down on the crest of a hill by light, medium, and high velocity artillery fire. The fire was hitting very close to us, and we could only cling to the ground and hope for the best.[10] Lieutenant Laudone and I moved out, hoping to find a safe place, but ended up with our heads in a culvert while shells hit the road above us. After the shelling stopped, we collected our party and very shakily made our way back to Kaiserbach, which we had missed on our way up. After some debate we finally followed another route and were able to reach Billingsbach and join Lieutenant Colonel Wisdom and his party.

Easy Company moved out to take Maad.[11] At 1750 we received orders to check Stocksberg and Jettenbach during the night, as well as to send a patrol to Prevorst. Patrols were sent out to do these tasks. Hot chow and additional supplies were expected from the rear, but I was the only one not on duty to wait up for it to arrive. It was midnight when the provisions arrived on a Weasel. The patrols returned without having reached their objectives and reported inconsequential information.

On the morning of 18 April, George Company went into Jettenbach at 0900. There was some sniper fire, and Lieutenant Heitman received a painful small arms wound in the fleshy part of his leg. On his way to the rear he received orders promoting him to Captain. Easy Company went into Klingen, and Fox Company started for Stocksberg. At 1200 Fox Company was in Stocksberg, and we received orders to cease our attack along the valley—that direction was leading us into the

ATTACK SOUTH

sector to the right—and to move to the east. The remainder of the battalion followed Fox Company into Stocksberg, where the vehicles and rear CP joined us, arriving by a different route. We then headed in column towards Prevorst, using a back trail. We were fortunate that we followed this trail as we later found the other routes had roadblocks set up on them. These other routes were also covered by prearranged concentrations of artillery fires along them and these concentrations were fired when we were heard in the woods.[12]

As we moved into Prevorst, a light artillery concentration fell around us, but we resisted the temptation to hit the ground and walked through it. At 1900 we were in Prevorst. I had assigned the FOs sectors for firing around the town, and we prepared to settle down in the schoolhouse for some sleep. Our vehicles soon joined us.

The nineteenth of April arrived, finding us in high spirits. It appeared that we were to get our much-delayed rest. The regimental shower unit was going to set up in our town. The Red Cross girls came up with coffee and doughnuts. We were told that we were in reserve, but one job remained to be done, and that was to check the only remaining village in our sector, Nassach. Easy Company was sent out to accomplish this task. Next we learned, indirectly, that Easy Company was in a firefight near the village and that German artillery fire was falling in Nassach. Before we had gotten all of the details of the firefight, we received orders to turn our sector over to another unit and to move to Gros Hochberg and Klein Hochberg. At 1800 Easy Company was ordered to disengage and to return to Prevorst.

The 2nd Battalion immediately started to leave Prevorst in column. As we knew of roadblocks along the route that the troops and tracked vehicles were to use, I joined Captain Purrington with his quartering party for a new rear CP, and we found another route to our destination. Captain Purrington returned to bring up the wheeled vehicles along that route, and I awaited the arrival of the main column. While coming up with the wheeled vehicles, Private Humpreys had an accident with his jeep. The troops arrived at 2215, and the CP and part of the battalion were put into Gros Hochberg. The rest of the battalion went into Klein Hochberg. As we waited for chow to arrive, the regimental liaison officer arrived with orders for us. He was not received very joyfully; we were worn out, it was well into the night, and we were to move out immediately to make a motorized flanking move during darkness. Orders were issued, but we were able to stay until we could have some of the hot chow.

At 0100 the morning of 20 April, the battalion was motorized to the extent of the transportation that the regiment could find and was on its way. Our move was to circle to the rear and the left, pass through recently captured Murrhardt, cross the Murr River and seize the high ground south and west of Murrhardt, and cover the regiment's crossing of the Murr River in the morning. As it was dark and the road information was very sketchy, I joined others of the battalion staff on road reconnaissance. I am sure that I was the first American to enter several towns before we found the right road and got to Murrhardt. As it was, part of the column did get on the wrong roads, but at 0600 Easy and George Companies jumped off,

ATTACK SOUTH

west of Murrhardt, toward Hill 553 (also called Siebenknie). I followed with my radio in the battalion command group. At 0730 we were on our objective without having encountered any resistance but well winded from our climb. After trying all night to reach the 374th FA Battalion CP by radio I finally was able to reach them for the first time. After a roadblock had been removed, our vehicles joined us, and at 1005 the battalion was assembled at Siebenknie.

After all of our efforts during the night, the regiment met no opposition in crossing the Murr River and moved rapidly forward. At 1730 we were ordered to come down off our hill and to follow through the sector, cleaning up and bypassing opposition. Such is the life of a reserve battalion! At 2000 we were closing into Unter Bruden for the night.

The twenty-first of April, a rainy, dreary day, was spent in checking more towns, using the tanks and TDs to carry riflemen to speed up the process. A small bridge fell in with one tank, and some infantrymen riding the tank were killed while others were injured. As we were about to settle down for the night, at 2100, we were ordered to make another night march, via Gerarstetten, Grunbach, and Beutelsbach, to the vicinity of Aishachies and to await orders in that place. I was able to drop in on the 374th FA Battalion's CP for a few minutes as the 2nd Battalion was reassembling for the move.

The start of 22 April, a Sunday, found us on the road waiting for the reduction of a roadblock. I was lucky on the move; I could ride and in the darkness heard an exchange between two tired foot soldiers about those who were able to ride. After the road block was cleared, we moved on to a road junction near Sckamback, where two rifle companies turned into Sckamback and the remainder of the battalion went on to Aishachies.

I arrived in Aishachies just behind the first squad to enter the town. It was near 0400, I was tired and looking forward to finding a bed. In the dark I found a lot of confusion. It turned out that the lead scouts had met a column of men in civilian clothes marching out of town in a military formation. On searching them they were found to be carrying pistols.[13] As our column went into town, they encountered German soldiers, and an organized house-to-house search was started. Soldiers were found to be still asleep in nearly every house. As the group of captives, which started with the marching civilians, grew, pistols started to drop. I took a Mauser pistol as my souvenir. It was 0615 when our column closed into the town. Lieutenant Colonel Wisdom and the staff officers soon retired; Lieutenant Clark also did, after he had lain claim to a variety of pistols from the pile being collected. I stayed to watch the prisoner collection grow. Two officers were brought in. One of the uniformed Wehrmacht enlisted men was a chubby youth who spoke English with a perfect Brooklyn accent—he drew some of our soldiers who wanted to talk with him, but that contact was broken up. I counted the POWs several times; when the number passed two hundred, I went to bed.

Later in the morning I was awakened to take a call from Major Allport. He asked if the 2nd Battalion could send some help to wipe out some bypassed

ATTACK SOUTH

resistance.[14] After considering the requirement of our mission and the shape that the battalion was in, Lieutenant Colonel Wisdom had to deny the requested help. Later I was able to find out that a 374th FA Battalion reconnaissance party had been ambushed. The survey section driver, Private Gibson, had been killed, and some others had been injured.[15] The rest of the day was spent in patrolling and recovering from our recent activities. When a detail came to pick up our prisoners, there were 225 POWs, with only a few of these from Sckamback. Most of them had been captured without a fight in our town by one rifle company, the weapons company, and the battalion headquarters company.[16]

On the twenty-third we were told to prepare for a motor movement. When trucks from the 373rd FA Battalion arrived, we were told to stand by for orders. Finally we were ordered to move to Zell on foot and the empty trucks to move there to meet us. The attached vehicles arrived in Zell ahead of the foot troops. Colonel Singles met me on the road and gave the order for the battalion to cross the Neckar and to clear the area between the river and the Autobahn as far west as Stuttgart. As no bridge could be seen remaining across the river, the battalion started across wading. With the accompanying wheeled vehicles, I went looking for a bridge and found one still intact. We went in search of the battalion, but the regimental S-2 met us and I was told to have the troops turn back and to assemble in Deizisau. After quite a bit of trying to contact the foot troops by radio, I finally got through to them; they were nearly at their objective. At 2030 the battalion was closed into the town of Deizisau, where their vehicles, including the kitchen trucks, were waiting for them.

The twenty-fourth of April saw jeep patrols conducted in our sector as the only aggressive act. The shower unit set up and did a big business in showers and clean clothes. On the twenty-fifth word reached us. We were now to assume the functions of the Army of Occupation. On the twenty-sixth I returned to the 374th FA Battalion and acted as the headquarters battery commanding officer/communications officer. The division was to move into Stuttgart, but the 374th FA Battalion could not find suitable billets in that bombed out city and moved on to the suburb of Sillenbach.

After several days of negotiations at the strategic level, the American troops were moved out of Stuttgart, and the French troops completed their take-over of the city. On 30 April this move took the 374th FA Battalion CP to Lorch. We were still in Lorch on 8 May when V-E Day arrived.

Notes

1. Every building exhibited a white display at each upper window. Some were cloths hanging down. Others were hung on flagstaffs. We supposed the flagstaffs to have previously displayed Nazi swastikas.

ATTACK SOUTH

2. We were quite startled when a scholarly looking woman stepped forward and asked in excellent English if our shoe soles were really rubber. Apparently the Germans were used to synthetic material instead of real rubber.

3. The bombing the day before had brought to the town's inhabitants a very late exposure to the realities of their war. After the intense fighting in Heilbronn, there was not much sympathy for them from our personnel.

4. Blackout discipline is not consistant with infantry combat conditions. Going from strong light into darkness spoils nighttime vision, but the lights being on did aggravate the enemy to take action to destroy the electrical distribution system.

5. The extensive bombing by TAC at this time may have been the desire to deplete their bomb inventories rather than have to move them to the Pacific Theater.

6. The use of bicycles for transportation gave us an indication of the state of the transportation in Germany at that time. Their lines of communications were quite short. Armored vehicles had priority over personnel transportation for a limited supply of fuel.

7. This was probably just a joke on me. Everyone knew of my desire to have a Lugar, and I never saw the one that supposedly was found near where I slept.

8. The SCR-694 was a battery-pack version of the SCR-610.

9. The AT Company is not later mentioned in my notes. The company may have gone back to a more conventional AT mission of providing roadblocks.

10. We did not count rounds or take other data for a shell report. So much for the training lectures about making observations during a shelling to calm one's fears!

11. Maad was just another small crossroad with a few buildings and a name. In the absence of any other designation, we used the German *Dorf.*

12. On the eighteenth, the 3rd Battalion, 399th Infantry engaged in an operation at Beilstein Castle and Fohlenberg Mountain, for which they were to receive, years later, a Distinguished Unit Citation.

13. By being in a military formation, these men in civilian clothing gave themselves away. What their status was under the Geneva Convention regulation might be interesting—could they be considered spies?

14. This request was not made through channels. It should have been addressed to regiment, the only command which could change the 2nd Battalion mission.

15. I regretted that I had not long ago arranged to have Private Gibson's PFC stripe restored. The act that caused me to take his stripe away warranted only a short period of punishment for the good soldier that he was.

16. I was too busy with the infantry moves to be concerned as to how the 374th FA Battalion managed to support the actions during this period of racing through Germany. It was a period of making rapid and frequent changes of positions for direct support artillery. Our 105mm howitzers had a maximum range of twelve thousand, five hundred yards (seven miles) to deliver their thirty-three-pound projectiles.

Glossary

AA Anti-aircraft fire ("ack-ack")
AAA Anti-aircraft artillery
AAC Army Air Corps
Able Phonetic letter A, as for Able Battery or Able Company
AFA Armored field artillery
AM Amplitude modulation (radio)
APO Army Post Office
Arty Artillery
ASN Army serial number
ASTP Army Special Training Program
AT Anti-tank
AW Automatic weapon
AWOL Absent Without Leave
Baker Phonetic letter B, as for Baker Battery or Baker Company
BAR Browning automatic rifle
Bazooka American 2.36-inch rocket launcher
BBC British Broadcasting Corporation
Blue Third Battalion designator
Bn Battalion
Bouncing Betty German spring-loaded anti-personnel mine
Btry Battery
Burp-gun German sub-machine gun, Schmisser MP-20
Cannon A shortened howitzer
Cap Captured
Cav Cavalry
CE Corps of Engineers
Charlie Phonetic letter C, as for Charlie Battery or Charlie Company
CIC Counter Intelligence Corps, US Army

GLOSSARY

CG Commanding general
Co Company
CO Commanding officer
Comm Communications
Commo Communications officer
CP Command post
Cpl Corporal
Det Detachment (e.g. Med. Det.)
Div Division
Dog Phonetic letter D, usually Dog Company
Dog tags Identification tags; strung together in pairs
DOW Died of wounds
DPs Displaced persons
Dragon's teeth Concrete pillars or iron posts erected as tank barriers
Draftee Drafted soldier
Easy Phonetic letter E, usually Easy Company
EM Enlisted man (men)
Enlistee Volunteer soldier
Eng Engineer
ETO European Theater of Operations
ExO Executive officer
FA Field artillery
FDC Fire Direction Center, Field Artillery Battalion Operations Center
FFI French Forces of the Interior
Flac Anti-aircraft fire
FM Frequency modulation (radio)
FO Forward observer
Fox Phonetic letter F, usually Fox Company
Foxhole Deep two-man entrenchment
George Phonetic letter G, usually George Company
GI Government issue, hence a slang name for a soldier
GIs Diarrhea; from gastro-intestinal
Grade Enlisted personnel level
GMT Greenwich Mean Time
GP Group
Grease Gun American sub-machine gun, .45 caliber
GRO Graves registration officer

GLOSSARY

HE High explosive
HMG Heavy machine gun
How Phonetic letter H, usually H Company
HQ Headquarters
Inf Infantry
IP Initial point
Item Phonetic letter I, usually I Company
I&E Information and Education; programs for leisure time
Jig Phonetic letter J (US Army does not use J as an unit designator)
K ration Individually packed meals, three field rations
KIA Killed in Action
King Phonetic letter K
LIA Lightly injured in action
Liaison Contact maintained between two units to ensure concerted action
LMG Light machine gun
LnO Liaison officer
Love Phonetic letter L, usually as in L Company
MAC Medical administrative officer
MD Medical department
Med Medical
Meemie See screaming meemie
MG Machine gun
MIA Missing in Action
mil Unit of angular measurement: 6400 in a circle.
Mike Phonetic letter M, usually as in M Company
M-1 American semiautomatic rifle (Garand)
MLR Main Line of Resistance; principle defense line
MOS Military occupation specialty
Mortar Short barrel gun firing high trajectories shells
Nan Phonetic alphabet letter N
NCO Non-commissioned officer
Neblewerfer German multi-barrel rocket launcher, 155, 210, or 300 mm
NG National Guard
Oboe Phonetic letter O
OCS Officer Candidate School
OD Olive drab, color of American wool uniform
OP Observation post

GLOSSARY

OPL Out-post Line, located in front of MLR
Outfit Military organization
Panzerfaust German hand held, one-shot, shaped charged anti-tank weapon
Panzerschreck German rocket-launcher, anti-tank weapon (similar to American bazooka)
Peter Phonetic letter P
PFC Private first class
POSIT Proximity fuse (artillery)
Potato Masher German percussion grenade with wooden handle
POW Prisoner of War
PTA Payment transfer authorization
Pvt Private
PX Post exchange
Queen Phonetic letter Q
QMC Quartermaster corps
RA Regular army
Rank Officer personnel level
RCN Reconnaissance
RCT Regimental combat team
Red First Battalion designator
Res Reserve
R&R Rest and recreation
Roger Phonetic letter R
ROTC Reserve Officers Training Corps
Schu Mine German anti-personnel mine
SCR Set, complete, radio (often, Signal Corps Radio)
Screaming Meemies American slang for Neblewerfer fire (WWII)
Sgt Sergeant
Shell rep Shell report; report details on incoming artillery fire
Shoe pacs Insulated winter boots with rubber soles and felt liners
SIW Self inflicted wound
SNAFU Situation normal, all fouled up
SP Self propelled
SOI Signal operating instructions
SOP Standard operating procedures
SS Schutzstaffel, German elite guard
S/Sgt Staff sergeant

GLOSSARY

Sugar Phonetic letter S
S-1 Personnel function
S-2 Intelligence function
S-3 Operations function
S-4 Supply function
S-5 Civil affair/military government function
TAC Tactical air corps
Tare Phonetic letter T
TF Task force
T/O & E Tables of organization and equipment
TOT Time-on-target; artillery fires timed to have all rounds on the target at once
Tree Burst Air burst of shells on contact with trees
T/Sgt Technical sergeant
T/4 Technician grade 4
T/5 Technician grade 5
Uncle Phonetic Letter U
USO United Service Organization; A civilian agency that provided entertainment, doughnut wagons, etc., to the soldiers
V-E Day Victory in Europe Day, 8 May 1945
Victor Phonetic letter V
VT Variable time fuse for artillery shells
Weasel Small American full-tracked vehicle
Wehrmacht German Armed Forces (literally, War Machine)
Westwall German border fortifications; called Siegfried Line by the Allies
WIA Wounded in action
William Phonetic letter W
W/TP Wireman/telephone operator
X-ray Phonetic letter X
Yoke Phonetic letter Y
Zebra Phonetic letter Z
ZI Zone of the Interior

Bibliography

REFERENCES

Unit Histories (used in revising text)

Bass, Michael A., ed. *The Story of the Century.* New York: Century Association, 1946.

Boston, Michael A., ed. *History of the 398th Infantry Regiment in World War II.* Washington: Infantry Journal, 1947.

Finkelstein, Samuel, ed. *The Regiment of the Century: The Story of the 397th Infantry Regiment.* Stuttgart: Union Druckerei, 1945.

Gurley, Frank, ed. *399th in Action with the 100th Infantry Division.* Stuttgart: 1945.

Past in Review: The History of the 374th Field Artillery Battalion, 100th Infantry Division. 1945.

Personal Accounts (Century Division personnel accounts, cited in notes.)

Angier, John C. III. *A 4F-r Goes to War with the 100th Division.* Bennington, VT: 1999.

Bowman, B. Lowery and Mosher, Paul F. *Company I—WWII Combat History.* Carrolton, Texas: 1997.

Fishpaw, Eli and Fishpaw, Bernice. *The Shavetail and the Army Nurse.* Deland, FL: 1988.

Gurley, Frank. *Into the Mountains Dark: A WWII Odyssey from Harvard Crimson to Infantry Blue.* Bedford, PA: Aegis, 2001.

Gluesenkamp, Lester G. *Combat, A Short Interval in the Life of a G.I. in World War II.* Alma, IL: 1994.

Hancock, Frank E. *An Improbable Machine Gunner*, 2nd Ed. Madison, AL: 1997.

Norman, Caldron R. *Whatever Happened to Company A?* Portland, OR: 1991.

Watson, William C. *First Class Privates.* Atlanta, GA: 1994.

BIBLIOGRAPHY

Supplementary Reading

Official Accounts

Clarke, Jeffrey J. and Robert Ross Smith. *Riviera to the Rhine.* Washington: 1993.

Cole, Hugh M. *The Lorraine Campaign.* Washington: 1950.

Greenfield, Kent Roberts, Robert R. Palmer, and Bell I. Wiley. *The Organization of Ground Combat Troops.* Washington: 1947.

MacDonald, Charles B. *The Last Offensive.* Washington: 1953.

Ibid., *The Seigfried Line Campaign,* Washington: 1963.

Palmer, Robert R., Bell I. Wiley, and William R. Keast. *The Procurement and Training of Ground Troops.* Washington: 1948.

Turner, John Frayn and Robert Jackson. *Destination Berchtesgaden, Story of the US Seventh Army in World War II.* New York: Scribner's, 1975.

Pictorials

Century (100) Division. *Pictorial Review.* Albert Lowe Enterprise, 1944.

Pictorial Record, the War Against Germany: Europe and Adjacent Areas. Washington: 1951.

Other Accounts

Bonn, Keith E. *When the Odds Were Even: The Vosges Mountains Campaign, Oct. 1944–Jan. 1995.* Navato, CA: Presidio Press, 1994.

Pommois, Lise. *Winter Storm.* Paducah, KY: 1991.

Whiting, Charles. *America's Forgotten Army, the Story of the U.S. Seventh.* Rockville Center, NY: Sarpadon, 1999.

Source Book

Forty, George. *US Army Handbook 1939–1945.* New York, NY: Barnes & Noble, 1998.

Behavior

Fussel, Paul. *Doing Battle: The Making of a Skeptic.* Back Bay Books, 1996.

Ibid. *Wartime: Understanding and Behavior in the Second World War.* New York: Oxford, 1989.

Marshall, Samuel Lyman Atwood. *Men Against Fire: the Problem of Battle Conduct.* Washington: Infantry Journal and New York: Morrow, 1947.

BIBLIOGRAPHY

BIBLIOGRAPHICAL NOTES

The material used in the References was selected from a larger field that included related material. Excluded were those accounts that were not directly relevant to the author's account, were based on old correspondence, were sterile due to over-editing, were striving to support a cause, were not related to the tactical view, or were in formal military style.

A collection of army-published newspapers was found to be useful in the recall of minor events. These included *The Century Sentinel, XXI Corps News, Fort Bragg Post, Stars and Stripes, The Hatchet, Army Times,* etc.

Much interesting material is to be found the in newsletters of the 100th Infantry Division Association, but this has not been cited due to the limited availability of these newsletters, and the usually fragmentary nature of the accounts.

Appendix A
Geography

I. MAPPING

A. General

The military operations of tactical units were made from maps that had scales showing feature accuracy suitable for light artillery fire and infantry weapons. Most maps were of a scale of 1:25,000. After Action Reports of infantry units at battalion and higher level were based on either 1:50,000 or 1,100,000 maps.

Civil and topographical military maps show details such as benchmarks, elevations, slopes, vegetation, etc. In WWII overlays were used over the maps that showed the military features such as weapons, military units, etc. (Road maps only show towns, roads, rivers, and civil borders.)

The maps used in the 100th Division history, *The Story of the Century*, were made from the maps still in official holdings and as they were used in supporting unit and individual citations. These are now our best source of information about the locations during WWII.

Black and white photocopies of the Army Map Service 1944 maps of the areas of interest to us in France and Germany are available. The France sheet numbered XXXVII-13, 1:50,000 scale, is for Bitche and includes Rimling. The Germany sheet, designated V-3, Karlsruhe, gives 1:100,000 scale coverage.

Modern French topographic maps are issued by IGN (Institut Geographique National). They are current at the date of issue, so they show features like new roads, power lines, and buildings that were not present in WWII.

Map grids vary from map issuer to map issuer. One feature that is common in all maps is the markings for latitude and longitude. In the case of the town of Rimling it had the coordinates of: 54 degrees 55 minutes North and 7 degrees 16 minutes East.

APPENDIX A: GEOGRAPHY

B. French Maps

1. Raon-L'Etape Area, November 1944
Mapwise this area is a challenge. The scale of maps of interest all seem to corner here, requiring three or four sheets to give complete coverage. The 1:100,000 scale IGN Serie Verte numbers 12, 23, and 31 provide modern coverage. The IGN TOP 25 Series coverage of this area includes 3616 OT, Le Donon.

2. Bitche Area, December 1944 to March 1945
In this region several sheets of 1:25,000 scale maps are required to show the extent of 100th Division activities. These include the IGN TOP 25 Series sheets: 3613 ET, Sarreguemines (shows Rimling); 3713 ET, Pas De Bitche; 3714 ET, La Petite Pierre; and 3814 ET, Haguenau, Wissembourg.
One 1:100,000 scale map provides full coverage. This is IGN Series Verte Number 12 (which also is the one that provides partial coverage of Raon-L'Etape).

3. Battle of Alsace
This 1945 map, issued by Pneu Michelin and repeatedly reissued as Number 104, is a 1:200,000 scale 1947 over printed map offering a very different view of the November to March period. With the accompanying text in both English and French, it gives the French version of the combat in that area. In this easily available map, the seriously damaged localities are circled and objectives important to the French are shown.

C. German Maps

The short time and the small area that the Century Division was engaged in tactical operations in Germany does not warrant extensive map coverage. Two modern topographical maps were found that cover the Neckar Valley. One is a 1:50,000 scale map of Heilbronn dated 1995. It is designated as the L 6920 Topographic Kart published by Landesvermessungsant Baden-Wurttemberg. The second is a 1:200,000 scale map of Stuttgart-Nord. It is designated the CC-7118 Topographic Kart.

Maps of modern Germany show expansion of towns and other indications of population growth and change from 1945. A system of autobahns and other thoroughfares cut across the region; however, topographic features that controlled WWII tactical situations have not changed.

APPENDIX A: GEOGRAPHY

II. FRANCE, LOCATIONS

A. Town of Raon-L'Etape

The town of Raon-L'Etape is in the Vosges Department, Lorraine Region of France. It is on the Meurthe River, where the Plaine River joins it. It is dominated on the north by a high wooded hill. In 1944 the town consisted of the area north and east of the Meurthe, and it had a population of 4,090 (1939 census). It was spread along the side of the Meurthe and on both sides of the Plaine River.

In mid July of 1944 two French girls informed their German soldier boyfriends about a meeting of French partisans in a café north of Raon. This resulted in the arrest and eventual deportation to Dachau of thirty young patriots.

In September of 1944 the pressures on the town by the Germans were stepped up because of partisan activities by the French and the preparation of the area for defense. The mayor and others were assassinated, and the abbot was arrested. Cars and radios were requisitioned. In mid-September the electric power was shut off at the power company; it was restored in August 1945.

In October trainloads of materials and factory equipment were appropriated and shipped to Germany. More requisitioning of property and arrests occurred. Minor bridges and footbridges, both on the Plaine and the Meurthe, were destroyed, and then the railroad bridge was blown up.

On 1 November the main bridge across the Meurthe was mined, then on the fourth it was accidentally blown up, causing much damage nearby and killing twenty German soldiers. On the eleventh the Germans left the town, except for nightly patrols. The Americans arrived on the nineteenth. The town had 57 burned houses, 89 dynamited buildings, and 437 blocks of flats damaged. All the public buildings were destroyed or had suffered serious damage.

The town has been awarded two Croix de Guerre, one for WWII and one for WWI. From late 1914 to the end of WWI, the front lines were static along the Meurthe River in this sector so that Raon-L'Etape had a long exposure to military activity during this period. The names of those who died in both wars are shown on plaques at the Hotel de Ville, listed by cause, e.g. military service, bombardment, atrocities, etc. (A commemorative plaque was placed nearby by the 100th Division Association.)

On the other side of the river was La Neauveville Les Raon. This town was not highly damaged during WWII. Its mayor and another man had to walk several kilometers to the west to find 100th Division troops to tell then that their town was free of Germans. In 1939 it had a population of about 3,000. The two towns were formed in the thirteenth century but were distinct and independent. The Meurthe separated them, and they were under different abbeys. Raon-L'Etape was the market town, and Neauveville was the rural community but had the local railroad station.

APPENDIX A: GEOGRAPHY

In 1947 the two towns combined, and the main bridge was rebuilt. The result was a new community with a population of 6,331. The present Raon-L'Etape has a population of about 8,000. It has been rebuilt and is quite modern and growing. Much is recognizable to those who were there in 1944, but building a better highway from Baccarat to Raon-L'Etape had made that area nearly unrecognizable. A major industry contributed by Le Neauveville is Amos & Co., a slipper factory which employs one thousand people, many doing piecework in their homes.

B. Region of Bitche (Pays de Bitche)

The region of Bitche is nearly cut off from the rest of Lorraine by Alsace to its east, south, and west. To the north it is bordered by the both the German Saarland state and the Rhineland-Pfalz (Palatinate) state. It joins the rest of Moselle at Sarreguemines.

The Region of Bitche is divided into three cantons. It can also be divided geographically into three zones. The civil and the geographical areas nearly coincide. The Canton de Volmunster is in the upper central part of the region. Its deep wooded valleys are carved in sandstone with a plateau where limestone still is present. It has the smallest population of the three cantons.

The Canton de Rohrbach Les Bitche is in the western part of the region. It is in an area of agriculture with no industry, with a limestone underlying rock. Generally it is flat with few trees.

The Canton de Bitche is in the eastern part of the region. It is in the Northern Vosges and is mostly covered by trees. It is an area of red sandstone mostly covered by the Parc Naturel des Vosges du Nord, a part of the Northern Vosges. It has the largest population of the three cantons.

The region is considered the Siberia of France, having the coldest winters in the country. Those who lived here remember the winter of 1944–45 as the coldest of any. At other times of the year the climate is quite mild and the fields are fertile.

As a border area the region's development had been shaped by military needs. In 1869 a railroad was built to facilitate the movement of troops along the frontier.

The region became part of Germany by treaty in 1871. It remained German until the end of WWI, when it became French. It was many miles behind the lines during WWI, and the region saw no combat action. Whichever nation controlled the region, however, used the Camp de Bitche as a training facility, and in WWII much of the nearby countryside was ravaged by the maneuvers of the German army.

During WWII the region also was known for its Maginot Line fortifications, which were designated the Ensemble de Bitche. The US Army issued a map, classified secret, with an overprint showing the location of the below ground features of the fortifications.

The German name for the region is Das Bitcherland.

The region is predominantly Catholic, with a scattering of Protestant villages.

APPENDIX A: GEOGRAPHY

C. Town of Bitche (Ville de Bitche)

The town of Bitche is in the Moselle Department, Lorraine Region of France. It is on the Horn River in northeastern France near the German Border. It is at the center of the Region of Bitche and the seat of the Canton of Bitche.

The town is built around the Citadel de Bitche, an obsolete fortress. The citadel was carved into the red stone rock of a small mountain peak. It was built in the seventeenth century at the site of the medieval castle of an early ruler. The top of the citadel is at an elevation of 364 meters, and the town elevation is 300 meters. The top peak is 400 meters long and averages 33 meters wide.

Since medieval times the town has been closely identified with military defenses. It saw its only real test in the war of 1870–1871. The support of the military is still an important part of its economy.

A large area north and east of the town is Camp de Bitche, or Camp Militaire de Bitche. The German name for it during WWII was Hindenburg Kaserne. It is the third largest military installation in France.

The town name in German is Bisch or Bitsch. The residents of the town are called Bitchois.

At the area atop the citadel is a plaque placed by the 100th Division Association. Also, a street in the town is named "Rue de la 100th Division."

The town has been awarded the Cross of the Legion d'Honneur as well as a Croix de Guerre with a palm, or two Croix de Guerre. One is for the two Franco-German Wars, and one is for WWII, when the Germans deported 41 Resistance fighters. In the 1944–45 action, 35 civilians were killed and 119 were wounded. The Americans liberated the town on 16 March, one hundred three days after the delays caused by the Ardennes and NORTHWIND actions. The town had 104 buildings destroyed and 696 others damaged in the actions here.

The Germans held the town from after France's capitulation in June 1940 until it was liberated in mid-March 1944. During WWI the front lines were many miles to the south. The total population in 1990 included a municipal population of 5,415 plus a military population of 1,923. The population associated with Camp Bitche varies.

On December 13, 1944, the shelling and bombing of the town and its citadel was started and continued until the town was liberated on 16 March. The town residents took shelter in the caves that comprise the interior of the citadel, with no source of heat. They spent a sad Christmas with artillery shelling and aerial bombardment killing several, including children.

Modern day Bitche has an economy based on tourists. Tours to the citadel and to Maginot Line fortresses are supplemented by a golf course and other recreation facilities. South of town is College de Bitche, or Saint Augustine, a boy's college for training secondary school teachers. The St. Joseph Hospital of Bitche serves the region. Bitche has a Protestant church in addition to the usual Catholic churches found throughout the region.

APPENDIX A: GEOGRAPHY

D. Village of Rimling

The village of Rimling (Rimlingen to the Germans) is in the Moselle Department, Lorraine Region of France. It is on the east-west route D. 34, between Volmunster and Sarreguemines. Just east of the town is the north-south route D. 84, which follows the valley of a north flowing stream.

The town is at an elevation of about three hundred twenty meters. That results in its being dominated by a ridge, which runs from north to south, west of the town. This ridge has minor peaks designated by the military as hills of their maximum elevation. Northwest of the town is Hill 394. Just west of the town is a height called le Schlietzen.* Southwest of the town is Hill 375, and south of the town is Hill 370.

Observation of activities on the bare slopes of the hilly terrain was excellent (weather permitting) for great distances across the valleys. The Germans held the highest point in the sector, Hill 394. In the town the highest observation point was in the church steeple, making it a target for shelling and bombing, but it also was used effectively by Lieutenant Howard as a strong point against German infantry.

The village was first liberated from the Germans in December 1944. It finally was liberated on February 15, 1945, by the 71st Infantry of the 44th Division. At the end of WWII the town was thoroughly demolished. Two photographs of its destruction may be found in Turner and Jackson's *Destination Berchtesgaden* on pages 128 and 134.

The village had a population of eight hundred in 1940 and in early 1945. It now has a population of five hundred. It is a poor agricultural commune in the Canton of Volmunster in the Region of Bitche.

The rural houses of the Alsace-Lorraine region in 1944-45 had red tile roofs supported by sloped wood frames. Thick outer walls were made of limestone, covered inside and out with stucco. (Each village had a stone quarry.) The houses all had at least a basement, main floor, and one upper floor. The floors and stairs were made of wood. Each dwelling usually had an attached barn, with the main level for animals and a loft for hay. The windows had thick shutters that could be latched open or shut. Heat was supplied by small ceramic wood-burning stoves. In wooded regions each village had a portion of the woods, managed by a forester and gleaned by the villagers for twigs for fuel. After years of occupation by the German army, wooden sheds and fences had been used for fuel.

After WWII most of the buildings were restored in their original configuration. Those along the west-most north-south were cleared away, and the corner of the east-west street running into it was rounded. Adjacent to the restored church (Saint

---

* The elevation of le Schleitzen is 375 meters. Since the minor peak just to its south is one of the same height, the northern one has been designated in some accounts by a name rather than as Hill 375.

APPENDIX A: GEOGRAPHY

Pierre) is a town memorial monument that includes an attached plaque remembering the 100th Division personnel who were involved there.

The site of Rimling is the richest in archeological remains in the entire Bitche region. Mentioned in the thirteenth century under the name Rymelingen, from the Germanic masculine name Rimilo and from the suffix -ing, the village has descended from a Carolingian villa. The village of Rimling is located at the crossroads of two ancient roads: the salt route from Marsal towards Deux-Ponts and the Rhine country; and the Lompartische Strasse, which traveled from Lombardy toward Flanders.

APPENDIX A: GEOGRAPHY

III. GERMANY, LOCATIONS

A. The Neckar Valley

The Neckar Valley is a branch of the Rhine Valley in Southern Germany. The Neckar River joins the Rhine River at Mannheim. It twists its way mostly east, then mostly southward. Its valley passes in a southeasterly direction through the university town of Heidelberg and on to Heilbronn, where it turns south towards Stuttgart. The valley's east rim includes the Lowenstein Mountains.

In 1945, after the combat at Heilbronn, our interest in it was only in the north and west stretches of the valley as we swept to the south. The 100th Division's right boundary was the Neckar.

At that time the valley only had one multilane road that ran from Heilbronn to Stuttgart. Autobahns that have been built since WWII cross the valley.

The Neckar Valley is located in the state of Baden-Wurttemberg, formerly know as Swabia.

B. City of Heilbronn

The city of Heilbronn is on the east side of the deep, swift-flowing Neckar River and connected to Neckargartach and Bockingen on the west by road and rail bridges. A canal from the river acts as a barrier west of the river. It is on flat, open ground at the river, but after about twelve hundred yards the terrain abruptly rises to high hills. In 1945 it was mainly an industrial city and a center for transportation by means of road, river, and rail. It has a population of 100,000.

The combat for the city in April 1945 leveled most buildings. A church steeple and another nearby tower were battered but remained standing. At present the city had been rebuilt and is again an industrial city and transportation center. The church and the nearby Rathaus have been rebuilt. Heilbronn is located in the present day state of Baden-Wurttemberg.

Appendix B
Organizations

I. THE 100TH INFANTRY DIVISION

A. History

The 100th Infantry Division (often called the Century Division) was activated at Fort Jackson, South Carolina, November 15, 1942. Based on a NCO cadre from the 76th Infantry Division and augmented by about five hundred personnel of the Task Force Army War Show (from the 29th Infantry Division), it was filled up with draftees, primarily from the New England States. Training was begun on December 28, 1942.

After months of training at Fort Jackson or in the Carolina Maneuver Area, on November 15, 1943, the division departed for the Tennessee Maneuver Area in the Cumberland Mountains. Starting on January 15, 1944, the division moved to Fort Bragg, North Carolina.

While at Fort Bragg the division supplied replacement for overseas units and trained new personnel. Before going overseas the division had furnished 14,787 replacements (the division strength going overseas was 14,353). In addition the division was host to several reviews held for dignitaries from nearby Washington D.C.

The division departed New York Harbor on October 5, 1944, for Marseille, France, and arrived there on October 20, 1944. It entered combat under the Seventh Army (part of the US Sixth Army Group). During combat it served in either the VI Corps or the XV Corps, and also briefly in the XXI Corps.

During its six months in combat in World War II, the Century Division earned the Rhineland, the Ardennes-Alsace, and the Central Europe battle streamers.

B. Composition

While overseas the 100th Division was organized and equipped according to change 4 of TO&E 7, dated September 1944. Its authorized manpower was 14,281: 747 officers, 44 warrant officers, and 13,490 enlisted men.

APPENDIX B: ORGANIZATIONS

The following is a listing of the major units in the division and their telephone designators.

100th Div. . . . . Freedom	373rd FA Bn. . . . . Fraser
100th Div. Arty. . . Francis	374th FA Bn. . . . . Frog
397th Inf. Reg. . . . Frolic	375th FA Bn. . . . . Fragment
398th Inf. Reg. . . . Frigate	925th FA Bn. . . . . Fringe
399th Inf. Reg. . . . Franklin	325th Eng. Bn. . . . Friar
325th Med. Bn. . . . Fracture	

The 100th Division was a triangular division. In a triangular infantry division operational teams are based on units of three. There are three rifle squads in a rifle platoon, three rifle platoons in a combat rifle company, three rifle companies in a combat infantry battalion, three infantry battalion in an infantry regiment, and three infantry regiments in a division. Each triad also has a headquarters supply unit and a combat support unit.

C. Employment

When in combat the 100th Division usually operated through three regimental combat teams (RCT). Each combat team consisted of an infantry regiment, a light field artillery battalion, a combat engineer company, a medial collection company, plus attached tank and tank destroyer companies.

Assignment of the tank and tank destroyer organizations varied as combat needs changed. The tank companies were equipped with the medium M4 Sherman tanks. The tank destroyer companies had either 76mm guns, or 3" guns, or 90mm guns.

The combat teams were supported through division by the combat and service elements of the division. This included the medium field artillery remaining under control of the 100th Division Artillery. The 373 FA Battalion was a medium artillery battalion, equipped with twelve 155mm howitzers, which fired ninety-five-pound shells for a maximum range of nearly seven miles. All infantry division artillery was truck drawn.

APPENDIX B: ORGANIZATIONS

II. THE 374TH FIELD ARTILLERY BATTALION

The 374th FA Battalion was an organic part of the 100th Division. In the structure of the division, it was subordinate to the commanding general, 100th Division Artillery. It was organized according to TO&E 6-25 as a light field artillery battalion and was equipped with twelve 105 howitzers. Three firing batteries had four howitzers in each.

The strength of the battalion was authorized to be 31 officers, 2 warrant officers and 488 enlisted men. Each firing battery had 100 personnel. Service Battery had 77. The medical detachment added 10, not in the above count. Headquarters and Headquarters Battery had 144.

The operations center for the battalion was the Fire Direction Center. The FDC converted the information relating to calls for the battalion's artillery fire into data that the firing batteries used to load, aim, and fire their howitzers.

III. A COMBAT INFANTRY BATTALION

A combat infantry battalion was organized according to TO&E 7-15, which authorized three rifle companies, a heavy weapons company, and one headquarters and headquarters company. Its total strength, including a medical detachment, was 37 officers and 868 enlisted men. There were three battalions in a regiment.

Each rifle company had three rifle platoons, a weapons platoon, and a company headquarters. A captain commanded it. The weapons platoon had a 60mm mortar section with two pieces and a light machine gun section with three pieces. The rifle platoons had three rifle squads, three Browning automatic rifle teams, and a platoon headquarters. The platoons were lead by lieutenants. The rifle squads were based on five riflemen and two scouts. The squads were lead by staff sergeants.

The heavy weapons company, commanded by a captain, had a company headquarters, two heavy machine gun platoons, and an 81mm mortar platoon. Each platoon was lead by a lieutenant. Each heavy machine gun platoon had two caliber .30 machine sections, headed by a sergeant, and consisting of two seven man squads. The 81mm mortar platoon was headed by a sergeant had three sections with two squads in each.

APPENDIX B: ORGANIZATIONS

IV. BATTALION TACTICAL UNITS

Both field artillery and infantry battalions are the basic tactical units for their combat arm. At this level all officers are assigned to the battalion.

With any army command during WWII there were distinctions. Enlisted Men were one of 11 grades:

> private
> private first class
> technician 5th grade
> corporal
> technician 4th grade
> sergeant
> technician 3rd grade
> staff sergeant
> technical sergeant
> first sergeant/master sergeant

Officers were one of 10 Ranks:

> 2nd lieutenant
> 1st lieutenant
> captain
> major
> lieutenant colonel
> colonel
> brigadier general
> major general
> lieutenant general
> general of the army

Appendix C
A Battle for Heilbronn

HEADQUARTERS 397th INFANTRY
Office of the Regimental Commander
A.P.O. 477 U.S. Army
9 August 1945

Subject: Citation of Unit
To: Commanding General, Seventh Army, APO 758, U.S. Army (Channels)

1. Under the provisions of Circular Number 333, War Department, 1943, it is recommended that 2nd Battalion, 397th Infantry, be cited in War Department General Orders for outstanding accomplishments in combat during the period 4–12 April 1945, at Heilbronn, Germany.

2. a. At 0700, 4 April 1945, the 2nd Battalion received an order to proceed from Furfeld, Germany, cross the Neckar River and seize the Northwest or factory district of the city of Heilbronn. The battalion reached Neckargartach, directly opposite Heilbronn on the west side of the river at 1200, and found that all bridges leading into Heilbronn had been demolished. Division engineers were called to move the battalion across the river in assault boats. Concentrations of enemy artillery and mortar fire began to fall in Neckargartach in this time.
   b. The original plan of attack called for E Company to cross the river at 1400, under cover of artillery, and establish a bridgehead to secure the crossing for the remainder of the battalion. F Company was to follow E Company and attack south with its right flank along the Neckar River. G Company was to remain on the Neckargartach side of the river initially as battalion reserve, prepare to cross the river on order.
   c. At 1400 on 4 April 1945, E Company, with one section of heavy machine guns from H Company attached, began crossing the Neckar River in assault boats. The increased activity at the river brought heavy concentrations of enemy artillery and mortar fire down on the sight of the crossing. In spite of this E Company reached the east side of the river with very few casualties. On the far side of the river E Company turned south toward the factory buildings 200 yards away.

APPENDIX C: A BATTLE FOR HEILBRONN

The enemy was ready and waiting with well-planned and well-coordinated automatic weapons. Disregarding these automatic weapons and the murderous cross fire, E Company overran the enemies dug in positions along the river bank, taking 60 prisoners and inflicting heavy casualties upon the enemy.

d. The defenses within the factory buildings were much more difficult to overcome. Strategically located automatic weapons denied all avenues of approach to the buildings. By 1700 the two leading platoons of E Company were pinned down and support platoon was maneuvering very slowly around the left flank. At 1830 a platoon leader of E Company with one squad of men gained entrance into a small factory building from which 81mm mortar fire could be adjusted on the stubborn enemy positions.

e. Company F, with a section of heavy machine guns from H Company attached, began crossing the Neckar River at 1600, 4 April 1945, under the same hostile fire from artillery and mortars that E Company had experienced. Minimum casualties were sustained during the actual crossing and the company assembled in a power plant on the east bank of the river to reorganize.

f. At 1800 F Company moved from the power plant with a mission of clearing the factory buildings along the river bank, thus hoping to relieve some of the pressure confronting E Company. The 3rd platoon of F Company was leading the attack toward a machine shop when they were stopped instantly by an enemy machine gun from the shop. A 60mm mortar and a bazooka were brought up and the first platoon moved around the right flank on the bank of the river. The enemy machine gun was put out of action after a hard battle and this platoon of F Company entered the shop, taking 32 prisoners.

g. Company G, with a platoon of heavy machine guns from H Company attached, crossed the Neckar River at 1730, 4 April 1945, and moved into the power plant on the east bank of the river as battalion reserve. The 81mm mortar platoon remained in position on the Neckargartach side of the river, where they were able to support the rifle companies with fire and where the supply of ammunition was facilitated. With all major units now across the river, the 2nd Battalion had gained a foothold in the fortress city of Heilbronn. The next 7 days were spent in dislodging the enemy from his fortified city, person by person, building by building, and block by block.

h. The enemy had every advantage of terrain and observation, Heilbronn being situated in a valley surrounded by hills on the north, east, and south. From these hills the enemy would observe all our movements and the excellent observation post afforded him accurate adjustment of artillery, mortars, and rockets. In addition he had knowledge of all tunnels leading to passageways in the hills and underground. He could move from the rubble of one building and by means of these tunnels come up in another spot and begin to fight all over again.

i. During the night of 4–5 April 1945, the enemy counterattacked from the south with an estimated battalion of infantry. The attack was preceded by a heavy concentration of artillery and rockets. E Company bore the brunt of the attack and

APPENDIX C: A BATTLE FOR HEILBRONN

was forced to give up some ground. One platoon leader was killed and many men injured by concussion grenades and panzerfaust. G Company was in position near the power plant behind E & F Companies to hold in case of a breakthrough. The enemy fought viciously and stubbornly and was determined in their efforts to drive the 2nd Battalion from the east side of the river. Anti-aircraft searchlights coordinated with accurate artillery and 81 mm mortar fire, adjusted by the Company Commander of F Company, did much in halting this enemy counterattack.

j. On the morning of 5 April 1945, E Company was held in position and reverted to battalion reserve. Casualties from the enemy action the previous night had weakened them considerably. The plan of action called for F & G Companies to continue the attack at 0600. F Company shifted directions slightly and attacked along the left, while G Company entered the fight on the right and advanced along the east bank of the Neckar River. F Company regained the ground lost by E Company, and captured a large three-story building before meeting any real resistance. Moving on this tall building, resistance increased and F Company's advance slowed down. The company commander's advance went to the top floor of the tall building to get better observation on the enemy position and while issuing an order to a platoon leader was killed by a sniper. F Company cleared another block and a half and was somewhat in advance of G Company. F Company was then ordered to hold in position and wait until G Company came abreast before advancing farther.

k. The first objective facing G Company on 5 April was a long, five-story factory, parallel to the river. The approach of this building was through a flat open yard. The 2nd platoon of G Company made their way into this yard and were immediately pinned down by rifle and machine gun fire from within the building and across the open yard. There was no way to maneuver this platoon forward or backward. The section of tanks was brought up into position on the west bank of the river directly opposite the long factory. Direct fire from the tanks demolished the factory and silenced the enemy opposing the G Company. G Company lost 9 men in this action and captured 29 prisoners in the factory besides killing and wounding a large number of the enemy. At 1415 G Company came abreast of F Company and the two companies cleared another block in each of their respective zones before dark. At this time F Company captured Captain Weiss, a battalion commander who was in charge of the Heilbronn defenses.

l. On the morning of 6 April 1945, an attempt was made to ferry tanks across the river on an engineer raft. A chemical company had placed smoke generators in position along the river during the night to conceal the ferry crossing. The attempt to get armored support to the infantry of the 2nd Battalion failed when the raft capsized and the tank capsized in the river.

m. F & G Companies, learning that armored support was not coming, prepared to conceal the attack, building by building, against the fanatic defenders of Heilbronn. Resistance against the exposed left flank of F Company was increasing and the continuous barrages of enemy artillery were making the progress very slow. The hill northeast of the city was smoked to cut off the enemy observation

APPENDIX C: A BATTLE FOR HEILBRONN

and units from Regimental Reserve Battalion were brought across the river to protect the left flank. This permitted F Company to concentrate all of its forces on the enemy resisting fiercely from an old salt factory. Under cover of one artillery concentration after another, F Company moved into the factory, killing 10 of the enemy and taking 54 prisoners. G Company was being held up in a group of wooden buildings along the river. Artillery, plus white phosphorus shells from bazookas, burned the buildings, enabling G Company to inflict a large number of casualties on the enemy and capture 24 prisoners.

n. During the night of 6–7 April 1945, considerable enemy armor activity was heard within the fortress city. Artillery, mortar, and rocket concentrations came into the 2nd Battalion zone in increased numbers. The engineers rebuilt their raft, and a jeep and an anti-tank gun were successfully ferried across the river. The anti-tank gun was put into position with E Company to protect to the north and east. Additional amounts of bazooka ammunition were stored in each company and bazooka teams were alerted throughout the night. An enemy counter attack supported by armor did come, but it was against another battalion in the southern part of Heilbronn.

o. Another attempt was made to get badly needed tanks to the 2nd Battalion. On the morning of 7 April 1945, two amphibious tanks were launched in the Neckar River. One would not start after getting into the water and the other could not climb the steep bank on the east side of the river.

p. F & G Companies continued the attack south toward the railroad. As they advanced, block by block, the threat of penetration from the east became an ever-increasing danger. To combat this threat E Company was placed in a blocking position to repel any enemy attempts to get in behind F & G Companies. At 1600 on 7 April 1945, E & F Companies received a large amount of direct fire from an 88mm gun situated on the high ground northeast of Heilbronn. A combination of smoke and artillery stopped this action and Company F was able to continue its advance. The third platoon was approaching a group of small, partly demolished buildings. Progress was slow due to the well-entrenched enemy in and about the rubble and debris. When the 3rd platoon was held up, the 2nd platoon of F Company maneuvered to the right and come toward their objective from G Company's zone. The enemy was caught in the cross fire between the two platoons and resistance ceased in this block.

q. Company G observed no visible activity in the tall green elevator, which was their first objective on 7 April 1945. A patrol of 6 men was sent to the rear of the elevator to find out if the building was being defended. The patrol captured three prisoners who informed company commander of G Company that the elevator contained 20 Germans and an officer. The elevator was partly demolished by heavy artillery fire and also a large number of bazooka rounds that G Company had shot into it. When the 3rd platoon of G Company did enter the elevator, they went in shooting and came out with 18 prisoners and 1 officer. At 1900 the 2nd Battalion was ordered to hold up in its present positions.

APPENDIX C: A BATTLE FOR HEILBRONN

r. During the day 8 April 1945, Company G had advanced a block ahead of Company F. G Company was receiving automatic fire from their front and also from their left at each attempt to move. F Company was concentrating on an office building being defended bitterly by enemy machine guns and overwhelming number of panzerfaust. With two platoons stopped astride a road leading up to the building and a third platoon mounting savage resistance on a flank, F Company was forced to withdraw slightly after sustaining quite a few casualties. Concentration after concentration was dumped on the office building until 1800. At dusk F Company was ready to go again. G Company supported this attack with fire and after a strenuous 2 hour struggle F Company was in possession of the bitterly contested building.

s. Several attempts were made to construct a pontoon bridge across the Neckar River between Neckargartach and Heilbronn. Each attempt was unsuccessful because of the intense and accurate enemy artillery, rockets, and mortars. Consequently all rations, ammunition, and supplies had to be taken across the river in boats and hand-carried to the fighting men of the 2nd Battalion. The small but dependable Battalion S-4 Section and the Battalion Ammunition and Pioneer Platoon crossed the river many times each night to ensure adequate distribution of essential supplies to the 2nd Battalion units. At 0200 on 9 April 1945, the supply personnel had carried supplies to the east bank of the river when they were caught in the most terrific nebelworfer (sic) barrage in the entire siege of Heilbronn. Several casualties resulted and several men were forced to swim the Neckar River to reach the west side. Badly-needed supplies were destroyed, which necessitated additional trips to the fortified city on the part of supply personnel.

t. F & G Companies were still 2 blocks from the railroad from which the 2nd Battalion was driving on the morning of 9 April 1945. Resistance was slightly intense, but the advance through the last two blocks to the railroad was costly to both companies. G Company drew fire from automatic weapons and snipers who had infiltrated into the aircraft parts of the factory situated on a peninsula, formed by the Neckar River and the Heilbronn Canal. F Company met only small groups of scattered resistance until they reached the railroad. At the railroad they ran into enemy riflemen dug in along the embankment, which slowed down their advance momentarily. Late in the afternoon 9 April 1945, 2nd Battalion units reached a railroad separating them from the southern bridgehead in Heilbronn.

u. The junction between the 2nd Battalion and the 1st Battalion was made at 1900 on 10 April 1945. A bridge had been constructed across the Neckar River in the sector of the southern bridgehead, enabling that battalion to get tank support. With the junction of the two battalions it was now possible to get armor to the companies of the 2nd Battalion. At 2130, 10 April 1945, ten civilians were encountered moving towards F Company lines. On questioning they stated that the Germans were massing troops in the hills north of Heilbronn in the vicinity of Neckarsaulm, preparatory to leaving. All during the night of 10–11 April enemy tank movement was heard to the north and east of besieged Heilbronn. Enemy

APPENDIX C: A BATTLE FOR HEILBRONN

artillery and rocket fire diminished greatly during the night in comparison to the 6 previous nights.

v. The sun rose on a different Heilbronn on the morning of 11 April 1945. Enemy artillery was almost nil and for all intents and purposes the great fortress city of Heilbronn was under control of the 2nd Battalion. With tank support, companies F & G moved east in line with E Company. In a coordinated drive all three companies attacked east as far as the Heilbronn-Neckarsaulm highway. Only scattered resistance was encountered, which surrendered under the numerical superiority of the oncoming battalion.

w. Early in the morning 12 April 1945, the 2nd Battalion cleared the remaining sections of the city and attacked the dominating heights of Wartberg Hill overlooking Heilbronn. The few remaining enemy were encountered and taken prisoner and by noon units of the 2nd Battalion occupied the hill. The battle for Heilbronn was over after a long, continuous, and costly struggle lasting eight days and nights.

x. With the first wave of E Company to cross the Neckar River on 4 April 1945 was a wire team from the Battalion Communications Platoon. This wire crew took a wire-head across the river so that the communication with units on opposite sides of the river was assured from the start. When G Company crossed another wire was laid, and a double line was maintained across the river for the entire eight days.

y. A switchboard and radio relay stations were established on the east side of the river on 5 April 1945, when the assaulting companies were only a few hundred yards beyond the riverbank. In spite of the terrific artillery, mortar, and rocket concentrations, night and day, the communications platoon maintained a communication between battalion headquarters and forward companies in a matter never excelled before.

z. The Battalion Aid Station was initially located on the west bank of the Neckar River when the 2nd Battalion began its assault on Heilbronn at 1400, 4 April 1945. Litter squads crossed the river with Company E & Company F evacuating the casualties in assault boats to the aid station. By mid-afternoon, casualties from these two companies were mounting on the east bank of the river and the intense shelling from enemy artillery and mortar at this crossing site was making evacuation more than difficult. To combat this, the aid station crossed the river and operated from the power plant, previously cleared, on the east side of the river. Aid men litter bearers evacuated wounded endlessly throughout the night of 4-5 April 1945, sustaining several casualties themselves. The following day a squad from the battalion Anti-Tank Platoon was disarmed and used as addition litter bearers to supplement the overtaxed medical personnel. Hour after hour and day after day, the litter bearers went after casualties over routes which were constantly under enemy small arms, automatic weapons, and artillery fire.

aa. The 2nd Battalion distinguished itself in battle by determination, heroism, and extraordinary gallantry performed under unusually adverse and hazardous conditions, which made it outstanding in the battle for Heilbronn, Germany.

APPENDIX C: A BATTLE FOR HEILBRONN

3.   a. Nature of terrain:
Flat; factory district of city, with large buildings interspersed with open areas. High ground on the northeast, east, and southeast, which overlooked the city was heavily wooded.

    b. Enemy morale:
Excellent; the enemy was determined to make the capture of Heilbronn as costly as possible, as it was the key to his system of defense.

    c. Morale of troops: Excellent.
    d. Weather: Clear and cool.
    e. Exact time and dates of action:
Action began 1400, 4 April 1945, and continued through 12 April 1945.

4.   a. Number of men assigned to unit cited who took part in action:
       Assigned: Off 32   EM 785
       Attached: Off 8   EM 78
    b. Number of casualties suffered by unit cited:
       Killed: Twenty-four   (24)   Off 2   EM 22
       Missing in Action: Five   (5)   Off 0   EM 5
       Wounded: Sixty-three   (63)   Off 0   EM 63

5.   a. Approximate strength of enemy: Two thousand (2000).
    b. Character of enemy fire and observation:
The enemy had excellent observation of the whole 2nd Battalion zone from Wartberg and pounded the crossing sites and the company's areas incessantly with all types of artillery, mortars, and rockets. Sniper fire was heavy, and large quantities of automatic weapons, panzerfaust, and grenades were used.

    c. Apparent enemy intentions were objectives:
The enemy intended to hold Heilbronn, which was the key to one of their main lines of resistance as well as an important rail center.

    d. Known enemy losses:
       Killed: 200
       Wounded: 400
       Prisoners: 500

6.   I have no personal knowledge of the facts stated in the recommendations. Colonel Gordon Singles, no longer with this unit, was regimental commander during this period.

                                                        RICHARD G. PRATHER
                                                          Colonel, 397th Infantry
                                                                  Commanding.

APPENDIX C: A BATTLE FOR HEILBRONN

HEADQUARTERS BATTERY 374TH FIELD ARTILLERY BATTALION
APO 447   U.S. ARMY

7 August 1945

The following is a roster of officers and enlisted men attached to the Second Battalion from 4 April to 12 April 1945 inclusive.

Capt. Curtis, Martin H.	HQ
Capt. Williams, Alton O.	HQ
2nd Lt. Moynahan, Peter C.	B
- - - - - -	
Sgt. Chany, Kalman J.	HQ
Tec 4, Bowler, Victor P.	B
Cpl. Pine, Donald D.	HQ
- - - - - -	
Tec 5, O'Rourke, Vincent A.	HQ
- - - - - -	
Pfc Collins, Warren G.	HQ (Then Pvt.)
Pfc Cooper, Lewis R.	HQ
- - - - - -	
Pfc Collins, Warren G.	HQ (Then Pvt.)
Pfc Cooper, Lewis R.	HQ
- - - - - -	
Pfc Humphreys, Bernard C.	B
Pvt. Collins, Warren G.	HQ

APPENDIX C: A BATTLE FOR HEILBRONN

STATEMENT OF RICHARD DRAUZ

I was educated by my parents honestly and faithfully, which had during all my life no ill effects.

I belonged to Adolph Hitler and Germany since my entry into the Nazi party with soul and heart. To act contrary to orders or not to fulfill orders was completely unknown to me. Therefore, I fulfilled all orders to the letter.

A great deal was written about the defense of Heilbronn and many conferences, mainly with Army officials were held. The defense of Heilbronn not only meant Heilbronn itself, but the whole Neckar-Enz defense in the Heilbronn sector, whereby Heilbronn was one of the key points in the defense system. The Neckar-Enz position started in vic. Grundelsheim and ended vic. Birkenfeld (Black Forest). The positions were started in the year 1935-36 and contained pillboxes, MG nests, and the like. It was not a continuous line of defense and led along the W slopes of the mountain ridge E of the Neckar and Enz. The plans for a breakthrough into the Kraichgental and also into the Karlsruhe/Heilbronn wedge because it was believed until a few year ago that the Black Forest, due to its natural obstacles and the Rhine in this vicinity, would be one of the most difficult obstacles. Therefore, the defense of Heilbronn was greatly talked about even before immediate danger existed. In the last minute, General Kitzinger, by direct order of the Fuhrer, had put into the hands of the party the improvement of the fortifications in the Neckar-Enz defense. Thus, the party was briefly occupied with military task of organization and training of the volkssturm (VS). The importance of Heilbronn in the Neckar-Enz defense was highly emphasized in that the training and equipping with weapons for the volkssturm was given high priority. Of a paper strength of 18 battalions, only 4 or 5 could poorly equipped with weapons and those only with booty (French rifles). Only the panzerfaust was available as a modern weapon.

The first two battalions which were trained in make-shift courses were committed in the Jegst and Kocher positions when there still was no immediate danger in that sector to complete training, which later proved successful; the 2 or 3 other battalions went into the Neckar-Enz positions.

Practically in all the villages, AT obstacles were built to stem the advance of the enemy. In the beginning, a mountain division was in the Heilbronn sector, which was very weak in strength. Later on, this division was replaced by a volksgrenadier division, but certain units of the mountain division stayed. The volkssturm was equipped with K98, French infantry rifles, and French LMG's. In modern weapons, only panzerfaust was available. Also, a few flame throwers were there, but they were never used.

My orders were: under all circumstances, together with the Army, to repel and defeat the most threatening attacks with my life and to suppress all subversive influence with all means I had at my disposal, in order not to allow the front to collapse. To gather returning soldiers from the sectors in which the VS was in position until withdrawing divisions could occupy the sector.

APPENDIX C: A BATTLE FOR HEILBRONN

I visited the VS battalions almost daily to supervise the training and the fortification of the position and to assist as far as possible. To the VS leaders, I explained daily their patriotic tasks. My own example caused them and their men to give their utmost. From three division commanders I received the verification that until they came to that sector on their withdrawal from the west front, they never encountered defensive positions which the VS battalions were ready to defend. I, myself, was always there where the fighting was going on and escaped a great many dangers. My own and my neighbor's house (Spahr) where the temporary office of the Kreisleit was located ever since the Kreisleitung was destroyed in the terror attack on 4 December 1944, because of several direct hits, damage, and artillery fire it was given up and moved to the Gaffenberg.

At the time when the Army started to occupy the sector of the VS the VS was under the jurisdiction of the Army, although the rations were received from the Party.

While bloody fighting was going on, on the Heilbronn front and the German soldier bled himself to death, there appeared behind the front irresponsible elements who hoisted the white flag to give the front the last dagger-thrust. According to orders of the high command, which appeared always in the press, radio, and special communiqué, those Germans were to be treated as traitors and to be shot immediately. I therefore, though with a heavy heart, had 14 men and women shot, regardless whether being party members or not. Amongst their city council were Hiebler and Taubenberger Sontheim. Taubenberger was still local party leader during war time, however, he was removed from office 1 to 2 years ago due to drunkenness and taking advantage of office toward the population.

The defense of Heilbronn was delayed until the moment when Divisions were pulled out to be committed at other critical points of the 1st Army. Thus, my task was finished, my belief in Germany's power and leadership was broken. Therefore I stopped all further fighting.

> I certify that the foregoing is a true translation of a statement made in German by Richard Drauz.
> /s/ Frederic Grunwald
> /t/ Frederic Grunwald
> Interpreter

Lists

Topics List

Aircraft
Campaigns
Combat team
Decorations
Distinctions
Distinguished Unit Citation
French Army
Lugar pistol
Mail
Mauser automatic
Mines
MOS
NORTHWIND
Phonetic alphabet
Rations
Rockets
Red Cross

Service medals
Shell reports
Smells
Sounds
SSN
Tanks
Time
Uniforms
United Service Organization
Volkssturm
Walther pistol
Weasel
Wehrmacht
Wire
   Barbed
   Telephone

Locations List

Achen
Aishachies
Alsace
Ardennes
Assenheim
Baccarat
Bas Rhin
Beilstein Castle
Bertrichamps
Bettviller
Beutelsbach
Bining
Bitche
Bockingen
Breidenbach
Bruche River
Brussels
Camp de Bitche
Chile
Colmar
Dachau
Deizisau
Dossenheim
Ensemble de Bitche
Erching
Ernolsheim
Etting
Etzlensmenden
Flexburg
Fohlenberg Mountain
Frohmuhl (e)

Furfeld
Gerarstetten
Grenoble
Gros Rederching
Gros Hochberg
Grunbach
Guiderkirch
Guising
Hantz Pass
Hasselthal
Hardt Mountains
Heilbronn
Horn River
Hottviller
Ingwiller
Kaiserbach
Karlsruhe
Klein Hochberg
Kleinmuhl
Klingen
La Chique Farm
Lehrensteinsfeld
Lorch
Lorraine
Lowenstein
Ludwigshafen
Maad
Maginot Line
Mannheim
Marseille
Melch

LOCATIONS LIST

Meruthe River
Moder River
Moselle
Mouterhouse
Moyenmoutier
Murrhardt
Murr River
Nassach
Neckar River
Neckargartach
Neckarsaulm
Neustadt
Niderviller
Niedersultzbach
Obr Heinriet
Oggersheim
Palatinate
Paris
Petit Rederching
Peterphilippe
Pirmasens
Plaine
Plaine River
Plaine de Valsch
Prevorst
Rambervillers
Raon-L'Etape
Reipertswiller
Rhine River
Rimling
Rohrbach
Rothbach
Saar
Saare-Union
Sarrebourg

St. Avold
St. Benoit
St. Blaise
St. Helens
Saverne
Sckamback
Schifferstadt
Schillersdorf
Schorbach
Schwalb River
Schweyen
Senones
Siebenknie
Siegfried Line
Sillenbach
Simserhof, Fort
Singling
Sinsheim
Stil
Stocksberg
Stuttgart
Tete Des Reclos
Unter Bruden
Unt Heinriet
Urmatt
Vorhof
Vosges Mountains
   High
   Low
Waldhausen
Weinsberg
Wingen-sur-Moder
Wurttemberg
Zell
Zweibrucken

Personnel List

Aber, Maj, John E.
Allport, Maj, Robert B.
Armstrong, S/Sgt., Samuel B.
Bell, Sgt., Leon F.
Beach, S/Sgt., Roy S.
Belser, 1st Lt., Adolph L.
Bowler, T/4, Victor P.
Bradshaw, 1st Lt., Carl H.
Brown, PFC, Grady H.
Busbee, 1st Lt., Thomas I.
Burress, Maj Gen, Withers A.
Cammeron, Maj, A.N.
Carey, T/Sgt., Charles F.
Chambliss, 2nd Lt., Preston
Chany, Sgt., Kalman
Chase, T/Sgt., William
Christobek, 2nd Lt., Anthony
Church, 2nd Lt., Herbert, Jr.
Clark, 1st Lt., Edward O.
Coggins, PFC, Gray M.
Coleman, Maj, Flemstead
Collins, Pvt., Warren G.
Cooper, Cpl., Lewis R.
Cortellino, PFC, Charles A.
Cuccinello, 1st Lt., Dominick
Denton, 1st Lt., Raymon E.
DeSpirit, T/5, Angelo
Devereaux, 1st Lt., William E. II
Drauz, Richard
Ellis, Col, William A.
Fishpaw, 1st Lt., Eli I.
Forman, S/Sgt., Max

Foster, Capt, Max W.
Garden, Capt, William A.
Gibson, PFC, Jessie F.
Greci, T/5, William F., Jr
Greene, Maj, Allen R.
Guthart, 1st Lt., Wendell
Heitman, 1st Lt., Fred F.
Henderson, 1st Lt., Howell C.
Hoover, 1st/Sgt., Carl A.
Humphreys, PFC, Bernard C.
Jackson, 1st Lt., Henry G. Jr
Jones, 1st Lt., Kenneth L.
Lafferty, 1st Lt., John D.
Laudone, 1st Lt., Vincent A.
Law, Capt, William J.
Liles, Lt. Col, Claude M.
Lind, Capt, Robert G.
Lull, T/5, Clyde
Maiale, Capt, Anthony J.
Martin, 2nd Lt., James D.
Matts, PFC, Fred
McAllister, 1st Lt., George N.
McGuire, Capt, WaLt.er R.
McCrumb, Maj, Ralph C.
Miller, B Gen, Maurice
Moseley, PFC, William H., Jr
Mounsey, Lt., Joe F.
Moynahan, S/Sgt., Peter C.
Murphy, B Gen, John B.
Nay, 2nd Lt., Robert E.
Newton, Capt, Herbert C.
Noel, 1st Lt., John C.

PERSONNEL LIST

Oakman, 1st Lt., William F.
Odell, Maj, Dorris B.
O'Rourke, T/5, Vincent A.
Outland, Maj, Arley L.
Perry, 1st Lt., William E. Jr.
Peterson, Pvt., Carl A.
Pine, Sgt., Donald D.
Purington, Capt, George I.
Rabinowitz, 1st Lt., Leo
Richey, Lt., John B.
RooseveLt., President, Franklin D.
Rosse, 2nd Lt., Frank J.
Ruggerio, S/Sgt., Michael
Rundell, Capt, Edmund L.
Saxton, 1st Lt., Rayford E.
Schlosser, 1st/Sgt., Charles W.
Servas, Cpl., Andrew J., Jr
Singles, Col, Gorden

Skivington, Capt.
Skokan, PFC, Frank M.
Slayline, 1st Lt., William
Smith, Pvt., Andrew
Smith, 1st Lt., Robert D.
Southard, Cpl., Warren G.
Stallworth, Capt, William E.
Sullivan, S/Sgt., Richard J.
Teeter, Capt, Bonner E.
Von Hegel, PFC, William B.
Wardell, Sgt., Lester C.
Williams, Capt, Alton
Willis, Cpl., Robert M.
Wilson, Capt, John P.
Wisdom, Maj, Wiley B.
Wisdom, Lt. Col, Wiley B.
Worth, Capt, Franklin, J.
Zieve, Capt, Leslie